FACET fb BOOKS

BIBLICAL SERIES — 21

John Reumann, General Editor

W9-ABZ-497

The Semitic Background of the Term "Mystery" in the New Testament

by RAYMOND E. BROWN, S.S.

FORTRESS PRESS   PHILADELPHIA

These chapters are substantially reproductions of articles which appeared originally as "The Pre-Christian Semitic Concept of 'Mystery'" in the *Catholic Biblical Quarterly*, 20 (1958), pp. 417-43, and "The Semitic Background of the New Testament *Mystērion*," Parts I and II, in *Biblica*, 39 (1958), pp. 426-48, and 40 (1959), pp. 70-87, and are reprinted here with permission of the editors.

456A69   Printed in U.S.A.   1-3047

Introduction

THE Greek term which can be rendered as "mystery" (*mystērion*)
occurs twenty-seven or twenty-eight times in the New Testament
(one reading, at I Corinthians 2:1, is textually uncertain). Since in
only one of these occurrences it is on the lips of Jesus—and that in
a passage (about the purpose of the parables) which has been
notoriously suspect, considered by many to reflect the thought of
the early church, Mark 4:11 and parallels—and since the vast
majority of occurrences, twenty in fact, are in the Pauline epistles,
it has often been presumed that this New Testament use of
"mystery" represents an intrusion into Christian vocabulary via Paul
of a word from the Greek world and a concept from the pagan
"mystery cults."

Careful investigators, however, have long pointed out that New
Testament usage of this term "mystery" has possible connections
also with Semitic words and themes in the book of Daniel and
other late Jewish writings of the Intertestamental Period. (The four
other New Testament occurrences are in a book in many ways like
Daniel, the Apocalypse of John.) The Rev. Raymond E. Brown,
in a dissertation at the Johns Hopkins University, Baltimore, in
1958, traced out all the references in the available literature, Old
Testament, Apocrypha, Pseudepigrapha, and the Qumran documents
(which were at that time becoming available for scholarly study).
In three articles published in periodicals in this country and in
Italy he summarized his findings—that there is a pre-Christian
Semitic background to the concept of "mystery"—and applied this
background to each of the twenty-eight New Testament occurrences
of the term *mystērion*. These articles are here reprinted, with some
revisions and additions by the author.

Father Brown is a priest of the Society of St. Sulpice ("S.S.," a congregation of secular priests, originally French, devoted especially to teaching in seminaries). Born in New York City, he was educated at Catholic University, Washington, D.C. (M.A., 1949); the Gregorian University, Rome; and St. Mary's Seminary and Pontifical University, Baltimore, Maryland, the oldest and largest American Catholic seminary (S.T.D., 1955). His dissertation there dealt with the *sensus plenior*—or "fuller meaning" assumed, by some, to be intended by God but not seen by the original author in Scripture, a deeper meaning to be grasped by study in light of further revelation or development in the understanding of revelation—a topic on which he has published several articles (see "For Further Reading," p. 70).

After a year at the American School of Oriental Research in Jerusalem, working on the Dead Sea Scrolls, Father Brown became Professor of Sacred Scripture at St. Mary's Seminary, Baltimore. In 1968 he was visiting professor in New Testament studies at Union Seminary, New York. In addition to a number of popular articles and commentaries (including Old Testament treatments of Deuteronomy and Daniel), he has published scholarly contributions in several learned journals on a variety of subjects, some of which have now been collected in a volume, *New Testament Essays* (1965), thus making Professor Brown one of the few to have provided a *Gesammelte Aufsätze* volume before reaching the age of forty! He is today best known for his much-praised and judicious commentary, now in progress, on the Fourth Gospel and the Epistles of John ("Anchor Bible"; vol. 1, 1966). His most recent book is a collection of expanded lectures and articles on the questions of how much the historical Jesus knew (about ordinary affairs, religious matters, the future, and his own mission) and whether the New Testament calls Jesus "God."

This latter topic reflects not only a concern on Father Brown's part with later Christian formulations, like that of the Council at Nicaea about Jesus, but also a participation in current ecumenical discussion (here, concerning the World Council of Churches' Amsterdam Confession of Jesus Christ "as God and Savior"). When he was chosen to address the World Council's Faith and Order Conference at Montreal in 1963 on ecclesiology—a significant meeting where Professor Ernst Käsemann of Tübingen was the Protestant counterpart, Father Brown was the first Roman Catholic ever to speak at such a program. A number of his essays reflect lively ecumenical issues, and he has been involved in interconfessional dialogue on both the national and international levels. He is also currently one of the editors of "The Jerome Biblical Commentary" (1968). At Uppsala in 1968 he was one of the two American Catholics elected to membership on the Faith and Order Commission of the World Council of Churches.

For this edition of his essays on "mystery," Father Brown has made a number of changes, updating the material and revising points of style for the format of Facet Books. Non-Catholic readers will note that books which are (for them) part of "the Apocrypha" are included within the canon of the Roman Catholic Church. Throughout, they will find a catholicity of spirit and knowledge, especially in the secondary literature cited, as well as a familiarity with the primary sources surveyed.

Lutheran Theological Seminary   JOHN REUMANN
Philadelphia
June 1968

ABBREVIATIONS

BIBLICAL LITERATURE

The usual English abbreviations are employed; the last book of the NT is cited as the Apocalypse or is abbreviated (in the notes) to "Rev." The following references are used for books in the Apocrypha (accounted canonical by Catholics):

II Macc. = II Maccabees

Wisd. Sol. = The Wisdom of Solomon

Sirach = Ecclesiasticus or the Wisdom of Jesus the Son of Sirach

For the Pseudepigrapha: The Testaments of the Twelve Patriarchs are cited as Testament of Reuben, Testament of Levi, etc. The book of IV Ezra (always cited thus) appears in the R.S.V. Apocrypha as part of II Esdras.

QUMRAN LITERATURE

Details on the publication of the Dead Sea Scrolls are conveniently given by J. A. Sanders, "Palestinian Manuscripts 1947-1967," *JBL*, 86 (1967), pp. 431-40.

CD = the Cairo Damascus Document

1QS = *Serek hay-yahad*, the "Rule of the Community," or Manual of Discipline, found in cave 1 at Qumran

1QH = *Hôdāyôt*, the Thanksgiving Hymns, scroll from cave 1

1QH Frag. = an additional fragment of the *hôdāyôt* from cave 1

1QM = *Milḥāmāh*, the War Scroll, from cave 1

4QMᵃ = first text of the *milḥāmāh* (War Scroll) from cave 4; see n. 76

1QpHab. = *pešer* (commentary) on Habakkuk, from cave 1

Gen. Apoc. = Apocryphon on Genesis, found in cave 1

1Q27 = the Book of Mysteries, text 27 from cave 1

1Q36 = text 36 from cave 1

4QSl 11*b* = text from cave 4 (other portions of Sl have been published as the "Angelic Liturgy"), see n. 88

JOURNALS AND OTHER PUBLICATIONS

AP = *Apocrypha and Pseudepigrapha of the Old Testament*, ed. R. H. Charles (Oxford: Clarendon, 1913, reprinted 1963). Two vols.

CBQ = *Catholic Biblical Quarterly*

JBL = *Journal of Biblical Literature*

JNES = *Journal of Near Eastern Studies*

NTS = *New Testament Studies*

RB = *Revue Biblique*

TDNT = *Theological Dictionary of the New Testament*, ed. Gerhard Kittel and G. Friedrich, tr. G. W. Bromiley (Grand Rapids: Eerdmans, 1964 ff.). The German *Theologisches Wörterbuch zum Neuen Testament* began appearing in 1933; hence the original date for articles cited from *TDNT* is considerably earlier than that of the English translation.

ZNW = *Zeitschrift für die Neutestamentliche Wissenschaft*

OTHER ABBREVIATIONS

OT = Old Testament

NT = New Testament

ms(s). = manuscript(s)

MT = Masoretic Text, the traditional, edited Hebrew text of the OT

LXX = (translation of the) Seventy (Septuagint), a Greek version of the OT

Contents

I

THE PRE-CHRISTIAN
SEMITIC CONCEPT OF "MYSTERY"

DESPITE all the scholarly interest in the Greek mystery religions and in the Pauline use of *mystērion*, there has been no really complete study of the background of the idea of mystery in pre-Christian Judaism.[1] Such a study now seems imperative in view of the Qumran material. We shall investigate the concept of "divine mysteries" as it occurs in three bodies of literature: (a) the OT, including the Apocrypha or deuterocanonical books (both the pre-exilic origins of the concept and its postexilic development); (b) the pseudepigraphical books of Enoch, II and III Baruch, and IV Ezra; (c) the Qumran literature. From this survey the reader should be able to appreciate the importance of the concept in Paul's time, and the type of theological raw material on which he may have drawn.[2]

[1] The *rāz* passages of Daniel 2 have been frequently considered as a possible background for the Pauline *mystērion*. D. Deden, in "Le 'Mystère' Paulinien," *Ephemerides Theologicae Lovanienses*, 13 (1936), pp. 403-42, covered a wider background including the OT wisdom literature, and his treatment remains one of the best. G. Bornkamm, in *"mystērion, myeō,"* TDNT 4, pp. 802-28, investigated briefly the pseudepigraphical literature, especially Enoch. Unfortunately he puts together citations from Ethiopic Enoch and the much later Hebrew Henoch. Some of the older studies, like R. Kittel's "Die hellenistische Mysterienreligion und das Alte Testament," *Beiträge zur Wissenschaft vom Alten Testament* (Neue Folge 7, 1924), suffer from early 20th-century ideas of comparative religion.
[2] This work is the outgrowth of the writer's dissertation on *The Semitic Background of the Pauline MYSTERION*, presented at the Johns Hopkins University, 1958. He is deeply indebted to Prof. William F. Albright who directed the work, and to Drs. Lambdin and Iwry who gave valuable assistance.

1. "Mysteries" in the Old Testament and Apocrypha

(a) *The Preexilic Picture of the Heavenly Assembly and Its Secrets*

One cannot begin this investigation simply by studying *mystērion* in the LXX and the corresponding Hebrew words it translates. Actually, *mystērion* appears only in the LXX translation of the postexilic books;[3] and even here it is accompanied by synonyms for "mystery" or "secrets" such as *krypta* and *apokrypha*. Rather, we must trace the idea of "mystery" in its historical development and through a variety of terms. We may begin with Hebrew *sôd*, a word which is never translated in the LXX by *mystērion*.[4] A glance at the Gesenius-Buhl and the Köhler-Baumgartner Hebrew dictionaries will show that the word has a wide semantic area: confidential talk, a circle of people in council, secrets. An interesting cognate in South Arabic, which both dictionaries neglect, suggests that the basic meaning is that of "council, assembly." In the Minean (South Arabian) inscriptions we find that the *mśwd* (*m* preformative of the root *śwd*—perhaps *maśwad*) played an important role in the government. It was a smaller council consisting of the king, the nobles, and the privileged classes.[5]

When we approach the early biblical uses of *sôd* with the idea of "council" or "assembly" in mind, we find that this meaning particularly fits the passages dealing with heavenly *sôd*. Following the suggestions of H. Wheeler Robinson,[6] many authors have stressed the importance of the notion of a heavenly assembly in

[3] *Mystērion* occurs some 21 times in the LXX: Tobit, Judith, Daniel, Sirach, II Maccabees, and Wisdom of Solomon. It normally represents *rāz*.
[4] In only one possible instance does *sôd-mystērion* appear: for the *swd* of the Hebrew Sirach 3:19, the Sinaiticus suppletor (S^c-a) has *mystērion*. Otherwise, to render *sôd* the LXX uses a variety of twelve terms.
The following are instances of hexaplaric rendering of *sôd* by *mystērion*:
Prov. 20:19—LXX omits; Theodotion, *mystērion*
Prov. 11:13 (identical with 20:19)—LXX, *boulē*; Symmachus, *mystērion*
Job 15:8—LXX, *syntagma*; Theodotion, *mystērion;* Symmachus, *homilia*
Ps. 24(25):14—LXX, *krataiōma*; Theodotion and Quinta, *mystērion*; Symmachus, *homilia*
In general, to render *sôd*, Symmachus prefers *homilia*; Aquila, *aporrētos*; the Peshitta frequently uses *'rāzâ*.
[5] N. Rhodokanakis, "Das öffentliche Leben in den alten südarabischen Staaten," *Handbuch der altarabischen Altertumskunde*, ed. by Ditlef Nielsen (Copenhagen: Nyt Nordisk, 1927), pp. 125-6.
[6] "The Council of Yahweh," *Journal of Theological Studies*, 45 (1944), pp. 151-7. There is a shorter form in his posthumously published *Inspiration and Revelation in the Old Testament* (Oxford: Clarendon, 1946), pp. 167-70. As Robinson wisely points out ("Council," p. 151), the heavenly council has been interpreted figuratively where often it was conceived of realistically.

early Semitic thought. We may call attention to two aspects of this assembly as it appears in pagan thought. In both the Babylonian[7] and the Ugaritic[8] literature there are references to an assembly of the gods that deliberates on the conduct of the universe. There are interesting similarities in the expressions used of these divine assemblies and those which occur in biblical references to the heavenly council of God and his angels.[9] Secondly, besides the mythological aspect, we should notice that the terminology used to describe the divine assemblies is that of the governing and judicial national assemblies.[10] Thus the ruling authority attributed

[7] Robinson, "Council," p. 152, n.1, suggests that the ultimate origin of the Hebrew conception of Yahweh's council is to be found in Babylonia. In the *Enuma Elish*, tablets III-IV, we see the assembly of the "good" gods selecting Marduk to lead the struggle against Tiamat and the assembly of the evil gods. For a detailed description of the Accadian *puḫur ilāni*, see Thorkild Jacobsen, "Primitive Democracy in Ancient Mesopotamia," *JNES*, 2 (1943), pp. 167-72.

[8] For the Ugaritic concept of El's court, see Frank M. Cross, Jr., "The Council of Yahweh in Second Isaiah," *JNES*, 12 (1953), p. 275.

[9] The first person plural passages in Genesis (e.g., Gen. 1:26, "Let us make man in our image and likeness") might be explained as God speaking to his heavenly council. Compare the Ugaritic Baal epic where Anath goes to El's pavilion at the source of the two rivers to consult with him, in the presence of the other gods, about Baal's death. Their decision on a successor is couched in the first plural: "Let us make so-and-so king" (C. Gordon, *Ugaritic Manual*, text 49,20: *nmlk*—read *namlik*, an aphel causative).

Another example is pointed out by Cross (cited above, n. 8), p. 275. In text 51: IV, 43-4, the gods say in unison: "Our king is a triumphant Baal; our judge above whom there is no one" (cf. Albright's translation in *Festschrift für Alfred Bertholet* [Tübingen: Mohr, 1950], p. 5). Compare this to the role of Yahweh in Ps. 82:1, "God has taken his place in the divine council; in the midst of the gods he judges."

[10] The Ugaritic term most frequently used is *pḫr 'ilm* (text 17,7) and *mpḫrt bn 'il* (2,17 and 107,3). This represents the same stem as the Accadian *puḫur ilāni*. Accadian *puḫru* is frequently used for a city council (Jacobsen (cited above, n. 7, pp. 162 ff.). Another term in both Hebrew and Ugaritic is *dôr* (Amos 8:14, where *dôr* is used for the pantheon of Beersheba; and Ugaritic text 2,17—*dr bn 'il*). Frank Neuberg, "An Unrecognized Meaning of Hebrew *Dôr*," *JNES*, 9 (1950), p. 216, suggests that originally *dôr* was used for the council of the clan or tribe. Still other terms for the heavenly council are *qāhāl* and *'ēdā* which are also titles for the assembly of Israel. Finally the term *mô'ēd* which appears in Isa. 14:13 is used for the governmental assembly in Phoenicia—the *mw'dt* or *mw'dwt* of the Egyptian Wen Amun report (11th cent.), as pointed out by John A. Wilson, "The Assembly of a Phoenician City," *JNES*, 4 (1945), p. 245.

We might add to this the evidence of the vocabulary used by the LXX to translate *sôd* where it is used of the heavenly assembly: the *syntagma* of Job 15:8 is used secularly for the constitution of a state; the *boulē* of Gen. 49:6 and Ps. 111:1 is the title of the Council of the 500 at Athens; the *synedrion* of Prov. 3:32 and Jer. 15:17 is the Sanhedrin of NT times; the *synagōgē* of Jer. 6:11 recalls the Great Synagogue of late Judaism.

to the divine assembly in its sphere of activity is similar to that of civic governing bodies in the natural order.

In the Bible, we find that the Israelites conceived of the sky as a solid firmament; above it was the palace of Yahweh where he and his council of heavenly advisors met to discuss the conduct of the universe.[11] These are no longer equal gods, but angels, "the sons of God."[12] Throughout the Bible there are many passages which describe the heavenly council; the introductory chapters of Job and Psalms 82 and 89 are among the best.[13] In all it is clear that Yahweh alone renders the final decree in the assembly; the role of the angels is, at most, to suggest and carry out. In the opening passage of Deutero-Isaiah we hear the subservient angels being ordered to console Israel on its return from the Exile.[14] In the vision of the heavenly court granted to Micaiah, son of Imlah (I Kings 22:19), the angels make suggestions, but nothing more. In Job they have not even that much to do, but stand by silently while God gives the orders. And in Isaiah 6:1 ff., the attitude of the seraphim is that of profound adoration.

The authority of the heavenly *sôd* to enact decrees concerning the conduct of the world[15] gave it practical importance in Hebrew life. The decisions on high were made known to the people by the prophet who was introduced by vision into the sessions of the *sôd*.

11 An ancient poetic description is Isa. 14:13 ff., where the tyrant's ambition to supplant God is described: he wants to climb the heavens above the stars and sit on the mount of the assembly (*har-mô'ēd*) in the recesses of the north.

12 Terminology such as *benê 'ēl* and *'ĕlōhîm* (Ps. 82:1) is explicable in the light of the pagan concept of the assembly of the gods which left its traces on the vocabulary of Hebrew poetry.

13 Also Deut. 33:2-3; see Frank M. Cross, Jr., and David N. Freedman, "The Blessing of Moses," *JBL*, 67 (1948), pp. 201-02, n. 19.

14 That the unexpressed agents of Isa. 40:1 are the angels of the heavenly council has been established independently by Cross (see above, n. 8) and by James Muilenburg, "Isaiah 40-66," in vol. 5 of *The Interpreter's Bible*, pp. 422-43.

15 We might emphasize that there are judicial connotations in the biblical heavenly assembly too. God acts as a judge among the angels in Ps. 82:1 (also see Isa. 24:21); the prologue of Job has a judicial element; in Zech. 3:1 the prophet sees Joshua and Satan disputing their case before the angel of God. Moreover, Cross points out that the description of the heavenly host as *standing* (*'ōmēd*) around the throne of God in I Kings 22:19 employs the same verb used to designate participation as a member in a law court. (See "Council" [cited above, n. 8], p. 274, n. 3.)

Isaiah's call in chapter 6 consists of his seeing a heavenly assembly where God is asking the angels: "Whom shall I send?" Isaiah volunteers and becomes the true emissary of God. When Micaiah (I Kings 22) is asked by the king of Israel to prophesy, he answers by telling what he saw in the heavenly assembly. Amos (3:7) announces almost as a proverb that God will surely not do anything "until he has revealed his *sôd* to his servants the prophets." In fact, to have stood and witnessed a heavenly council became a criterion for distinguishing the true prophet from the false. Jeremiah warns the people not to listen to the false prophets: "For which of them has stood in the *sôd* of Yahweh, and seen and heard his word?"[16] We encounter the same idea in Job: Eliphaz asks him sarcastically, "Do you listen in on the *sôd* of God, and has wisdom been revealed to you?"[17]

This understanding of *sôd* as the secret heavenly assembly to which the prophets were admitted to hear its decrees helps us to understand the other connotations which the word has in Hebrew. Besides referring to an assembly in heaven (or on earth[18]), *sôd* conveys the notion of intimate friendship.[19] This is not too great a step, since anyone admitted to such assemblies would share a special intimacy with the others present. *Sôd* also came to be used for the secret decision rendered at such councils, and for counsel in general.[20] It is this last semantic step that interests us, for in the Hebrew represented by Proverbs, Sirach, and Qumran, *sôd* is used simply for secrets or mysteries.[21]

In the postexilic Jewish literature which we are about to treat,

16 Jer. 23:18 (reading a *waw*-consecutive with the versions). Also see Jer. 23:22.

17 Job 15:8 (reading *tiggāleh* with the Peshitta). MT reads: ". . . and do you monopolize (*tigra'*) wisdom for yourself?"

18 The earthly *sôd* may be an assembly of the righteous (Ps. 111:1; Ezek. 13:9) or of the evil (Jer. 15:17, 6:11; Ps. 64:3; Gen. 49:6). For *sôd* as the circle of village men getting together every night at the entrance of the town, see L. Köhler, *Hebrew Man* (Nashville: Abingdon, 1956), pp. 84-88.

19 Ps. 55:15, 25:14; Prov. 3:32; Sirach 6:6; Job 29:4. The culmination of this usage is found in the denominative verb *swd* (mostly hithpa'el) which appears in Sirach in the sense of "be intimate with," e.g., "Do not be intimate with a chorus girl" (Sirach 9:4).

20 Prov. 15:22; Ps. 83:4.

21 We shall have several examples of *sôd* used for heavenly mysteries later. In Prov. 11:13 (see n. 4 above); 25:9; Sirach 8:17, *sôd* is a purely human secret.

the knowledge of heavenly mysteries (*rāz*[22] or *sôd* and more rarely *nistār*[23]) granted to privileged individuals plays an important role. We believe that the background of such a concept is that of the prophets being introduced into the heavenly assembly and gaining a knowledge of its secret decrees. The fact that *sôd* is used both for the heavenly assembly and divine mysteries provides an interesting clue to the development of the concept.

(b) *"Mysteries" in the Postexilic Books*

We may make a transition to this section with a citation from Deuteronomy which governed the Hebrew attitude toward the secrets of God: "What is hidden pertains to the Lord our God, but what is revealed is for us and for our children."[24] This sets the principle that the divine mysteries lie outside the proper field of human endeavor.[25] Nevertheless, it was recognized that occasionally

[22] *Rāz* is almost certainly a Persian loan word in Aramaic and Hebrew (although in the Persian literature that we presently possess *rāz* does not appear until the Pahlavi period, and we can only infer its existence in the earlier language). See J. Scheftelowitz, "Zur Kritik des griechischen und des massoretischen Buches Esther," *Monatsschrift für Geschichte und Wissenschaften des Judenthums*, 47 (1903), p. 311; and S. Telgedi, "Essai sur la phonétique des emprunts iraniens en Araméen talmudique," *Journal Asiatique*, 226 (1935), pp. 254-55. In the OT *rāz* first appears in the Aramaic of Daniel, which we date to early second century B.C. If the *mystērion* of Tobit 12:7 represents an original Aramaic *rāz*, we would have a fourth-century occurrence at the latest. A still earlier possibility is the suggestion that a lacuna in the Aramaic version of Aḥiqar, line 141 (A. Cowley, *Aramaic Papyri of the Fifth Century B.C.* [Oxford: Clarendon, 1923], pp. 217 and 224) be filled with *rz* because there is space for only two or three letters, and the context seems to require the meaning of "secret."

[23] This niphal participle of *str* (for the biform *ztr* in Ugaritic, see W. F. Albright, *Bulletin of the American Schools of Oriental Research*, 94:35, n. 30) is not to be confused with the *mistêrîn* of Rabbinic Hebrew. The latter is a loan word from *mystērion*, as *teth* shows (although by failure to pronounce correctly, it may have been connected to the root *str* in popular etymology).

[24] Deut. 29:28, *hnstrt lyhwh 'lhynw whnglt lnw wlbnynw.* However, as P. Skehan has pointed out to us, there is a possibility that this means just the opposite of what it seems to say. The Masoretes put points over the last two words, indicating some doubt about authenticity. Perhaps *lyhwh 'lhynw* were the real words to be marked, but out of piety the points were placed elsewhere. If this should be right, then the text would read: "Both what is hidden and what is revealed is for us and our children." Cf. Wisd. Sol. 7:21 and IV Ezra 14:26.

[25] Prov. 30:3-4 supplies an example of the general attitude toward the rare privilege of participating in the council of the holy ones: "I have not learned wisdom, nor do I know the holy ones. Who has gone up to heaven and come down?" W. F. Albright, "The Biblical Tribe of Massa'," *Studi Orientalistici in onore di Levi Della Vida* (Rome, 1956), I, pp. 9-10, suggests that the original background of this passage was a pagan poem of *c.* tenth century B.C.

God chooses to reveal his mysteries to men, and in the postexilic period there were individuals who professed to have been introduced in vision to the secrets of God. Their resultant knowledge (no longer primarily a divine message to reform, as in the case of the prophets) covers a fascinating variety of "hidden things."

We may pass over the use of *mystērion* in Tobit 12:7, 11, and Judith 2:2[26] where the term is purely secular, referring to the political confidences of the king, except to notice that not every mention of *mystērion* need have religious connotations.[27] Nevertheless in the same chapter 12 of Tobit we have some important information which also bears on divine secrets. In 12:15 the angel who speaks identifies himself as one of "the seven holy angels who offer up the prayers of God's people, and go into the presence of the Holy One." It is as such a confidant in the divine court that he reveals the works of God to Tobit and his son. And what he reveals concerns God's plan for the salvation of the just: because Tobit practiced charity, God cured him. We shall see fully developed in the Pseudepigrapha the notion of divine secrets which refer to the retribution and reward of men.

When we come to Daniel, we have a whole series of references to *mystērion,* again in connection with a king, but with religious overtones. In chapter 2 we are told of Nebuchadnezzar's dream which he required the soothsayers both to make known and to interpret. All failed, but to Daniel (2:19) "there was revealed the *mystērion* in a vision of the night." In this chapter *mystērion* is used eight times, always translating the Aramaic *rāz,* to refer both to the dream and to its contents; for the dream itself is a series of complicated symbols which envelop a further mystery: the future of the kingdom. As 2:27-29 points out, no wise man could tell the secret; but "there is a God in heaven who reveals secrets . . . and he who reveals secrets makes known to you what shall be." And so here we have *mystērion* as we shall see it so often: a vision of the future revealed to man by God in figures; and both the vision and the

---

[26] The political secret also appears in the Vulgate of Judith 10:13; and in II Macc. 13:21.

[27] Whence the rashness of the statement by Joh. Schneider, " *'Mystērion'* im Neuen Testament," *Theologische Studien und Kritiken,* 104 (1932), p. 257, that the use of *mystērion* to translate *rāz* in Daniel was doubtlessly influenced by the Greek mystery religions. More likely, with J. A. Robinson, *St. Paul's Epistle to the Ephesians* (London: Macmillan, 1904), p. 235, the LXX translators were sparing in their use of *mystērion* in religious contexts because of the possible pagan connotations of the word.

interpretation are the work of God, who "reveals things deep and secret; he knows what is in the darkness and with him dwells the light."[28] The means of revelation will often be an angel; in Daniel's case it is done directly. As the king says to him: "I know that the spirit of the holy God [gods?] is in you, and no *mystērion* is a difficulty [Greek: impossible] for you."[29] In evaluating the evidence of Daniel, Bornkamm[30] says that here for the first time *mystērion* has the sense of an eschatological mystery: a veiled announcement of future events predetermined by God, whose unveiling and real meaning is reserved to God alone and the one inspired by his spirit. While this may be true of the *word mystērion*, actually we have here only a development of the more ancient concept of the prophet's introduction into the heavenly assembly and hearing there what God planned to do. The manner of revelation is different (symbols are now used as a vehicle of the message); but basically God's action toward Daniel corresponds with Amos' dictum (3:7), i.e., God is revealing his *sôd* to his servants the prophets.

In Sirach (early second century) we are told again that the secrets of God lie beyond human knowledge (11:4): "Marvelous are the works of the Lord, and hidden from men are his deeds." (The context makes clear that deeds include the vicissitudes of life and the workings of divine providence.) Since this is the case, the very practical advice is given: "Do not investigate what is beyond your powers; attend to what is committed to you, for what is hidden is not your concern."[31] However, at times God does reveal his

28 Dan. 2:22. The word for secrets is *mstrt'*—the only example in the chapter where "secret" is not rendered by *rāz-mystērion*. For a similar idea, see the Susanna story, v. 42 (Vulgate Dan. 13:42): "Eternal God who knows what is hidden (*krypta*), who discerns all things ere they happen." 29 Dan. 4:6 (Aramaic; R.S.V., 4:9). J. A. Montgomery, *The Book of Daniel* (ICC, 1927), p. 225, insists that the plural *'lhyn qdysyn* is not polytheistic but just an Aramaization of *'lhym*.
30 *TDNT*, "*mystērion*" (article cited above, n. 1), pp. 814-5.
31 Sirach 3:21-22: *krypta-nistārôt*. Please note that, for the Hebrew text, we are following R. Smend, *Die Weisheit des Jesus Sirach* (3 vols.; Berlin: Reimer, 1906-7) which reproduces the text of the first four medieval mss. found (none of our passages occur in the fifth ms., published 1931). At Qumran, the two Hebrew fragments from cave 2 covering Sirach 6:20-31 help to vouch for the basic authenticity of the medieval copies (see M. Baillet, *Discoveries in the Judean Desert, III* [Oxford: Clarendon Press, 1962], pp. 75-77). The text of Sir. 39:27–44:17 has been published by Y. Yadin, *The Ben Sira Scroll from Masada* (Jerusalem: Israel Exploration Society, 1965); and that of 51:13-20, 30 by J. A. Sanders, *Discoveries in the Judean Desert, IV* (Oxford: Clarendon Press, 1965), cols. 21-22. The best general discussion is A. DiLella, *The Hebrew Text of Sirach* (The Hague: Mouton, 1966).

secrets, especially to the humble.[32] One great example of this was Isaiah, "who looked into the future by a powerful spirit," and foretold "hidden things [*apokrypha*] not yet fulfilled" (Sirach 48: 24-25). It is in Sirach that for the first time we meet Wisdom as an agent of God in revealing mysteries. When Wisdom is convinced of the goodness of a stranger, she comes to him, brings him happiness, and "reveals her secrets [*krypta*] to him" (Sirach 4:18).[33] We shall discuss the role of Wisdom more fully in dealing with the Wisdom of Solomon.

We should notice some very important facets of the heavenly secrets that appear in Sirach: (a) The mysteries of God can concern the natural phenomena in the universe. Chapter 43 describes the beauty of the sun, moon, stars, clouds, storms, and various forms of precipitation. It concludes with the words: "There are many secrets [*apokrypha*] yet greater than these, for we [or I] have seen but a few of His works."[34] (b) Secrets can be applied to the actions of men, especially evil actions done in secrecy which shall be revealed by God in due time.[35] (c) Sirach seems to teach that a knowledge of the secrets of God can be obtained through studying the ancient traditions. Chapter 39 begins with praise for the man who applies himself to study the law of Moses, the wisdom of the ancients, and prophecies—the three divisions of the Hebrew Bible, with the wisdom books in the second place. In addition to the written tradition, one must study the wise sayings preserved in the óral tradition (39:2-3): "He conserves the discourses of famous men and penetrates the intricacies of parables; he searches out the

[32] Sirach 42:18-19: "The Most High . . . makes known the past and the future, and reveals the path of hidden things [*apokrypha-nistārôt*]." Also Sir. 3:19 (the additional line in the Heb. and the Sinaiticus suppletor[c-a]): ". . . it is to the humble that he reveals his secrets [*mystēria-sôdāw*]."
[33] Also Sirach 14:20-21: Happy is the man who meditates on Wisdom and "reflects on her secrets (?)." The LXX has *apokrypha* which implies Heb. *nistārôt;* the present Heb. reading *tbwnt,* "skills," is, as pointed out by Smend (cited above, n. 31), II, p. 137, probably vertical dittography from the same word in v. 20. The Peshitta (*šbyl*) implies the reading *ntybwt,* "paths."

Another important text is Sirach 24:2. Here Wisdom "opens her mouth in the assembly of the Most High," and tells the story of her origin. The Heb. is not preserved, but in this context of the heavenly assembly, the LXX *ekklēsia* may well render an original *sôd*. This text is doubly interesting since in Wisd. Sol. 6:22 the origin of Wisdom is specifically called a mystery (see below).
[34] Sirach 43:32, following the LXX. The Hebrew is incomplete. Smend reads *npl',* "marvel," in place of "secret"; but N. Peters, *Der hebräische Text des Buches Ecclesiasticus* (Freiburg: Herder, 1902), p. 404, reads *nstrwt.*
[35] Sirach 1:30. For God's ability to penetrate the secret wickedness of sinners, see 16:17 ff.; 17:15 ff.; 23:18 ff.; 39:19.

secrets [*apokrypha*] of proverbs and is busy with the hidden meanings [*ainigmata*] of parables."[36] If it pleases God, this man will be filled with understanding, and will be able to direct his own knowledge and "will meditate on His mysteries [*apokrypha*]."[37]

When we turn to the Wisdom of Solomon, we encounter a deuterocanonical book which was originally composed in Greek by an Alexandrian Jew (early first century B.C.?) and bears the imprint of its Hellenistic milieu.[38] There are several interesting references to divine mysteries. The author warns against the ways of the wicked who have erred: "And they knew not the secrets [*mystēria*] of God; neither did they hope for a recompense of holiness" (Wisd. Sol. 2:22). The context, describing how the foolish think that the life of the blessed ends with death, makes clear that God's secrets here refer to his plans for the after-life.[39]

To enlighten men, the author says (6:22): "Now what Wisdom is and how she came to be I shall relate, and I shall not hide mysteries from you. But from the beginning of creation I shall search out and bring to light knowledge of her." This text has caused a great deal of debate. As Weber[40] points out, many authors interpret it as a jibe at the pagan mystery religions which hid their mysteries for the select few. However, H. A. Wolfson[41] has observed that even in the pagan world "mysteries," besides referring to religious rites, referred also to that type of wisdom which belonged only to the gods and was imparted in secret only to a few. In his interpretation, 6:22 is in opposition to this more general type of mystery, and not to the mystery religions. We would only add that the employment of the term *mystērion* in this passage is not particularly startling since the emanation of Wisdom from

[36] To this we might add Sirach 47:15-17: the praise of Solomon as a fashioner of wise sayings and "puzzling parables (*parabolai ainigmatōn*)." For Sirach the riddles or proverbs seem to hide divine mysteries.
[37] Sirach 39:7 (no Hebrew). In the LXX the "His" seems to refer to God; Smend (cited above, n. 31), II, p. 355, would emend this and make the pronoun refer to Wisdom.
[38] J. Weber, *La Sagesse* (Pirot-Clamer Bible, vol. VI, 1941), p. 367: "The author was not content to enunciate the doctrine received from the ancients in traditional language, but rather attempted to translate it into philosophical terms." However, as noted by J. Reider, *The Book of Wisdom* (Dropsie College, Jewish Apocryphal Literature series, 1957), p. 37, there is no evidence here of a profound grasp of Greek philosophy, but only a popular use of its terms.
[39] So Weber (cited above, n. 38), p. 415. Yet Reider, (cited above, n. 38), p. 69, n. 22, says that some understand these mysteries as referring to God's dealings on this earth.
[40] *La Sagesse* (cited above, n. 38), p. 422.
[41] *Philo* (Cambridge: Harvard University Press, 1948), I, pp. 24-26.

God[42] took place unseen by man, and therefore it could well be called secret without any definite adversary in mind.

When we pass on to other texts in the Wisdom of Solomon, we do meet some terminology which suggests a familiarity with language used by the mystery cults. We may distinguish two different usages: (a) The application of mystery-religion terminology to pagan rituals of past Israelite history (a process akin to applying the terminology of modern warfare, e.g., "blitzkrieg," to Joshua's attack on Canaan). For instance, Wisd. Sol. 12:5, in describing the initiates of Canaanite orgies, uses the term *mystēs*. This type of usage is found in the LXX and the later Greek translations[43] and is certainly not peculiar to the Wisdom of Solomon. (b) The application of mystery terminology to describe contemporary events or to express the religious thought of the writer. If we are not mistaken, this usage is peculiar to the Wisdom of Solomon. In Wisd. Sol. 14:15 the writer tells how a pagan father, bereaved at the loss of his son, established a cult of the dead: "And the former dead man he now honors as a god, and hands down to his adherents mysteries and rites [*mystēria, teletai*]." The chapter continues, speaking of pagan "rites [*teletai*] of child-murder," and "secret mysteries [*mystēria*]" and "frenzied carousals [*kōmoi*—Bacchic processions] of strange ritual." It seems reasonably certain that here the object of the writer's scorn was some debased form of mystery cult. When we turn to the use of this terminology for the writer's own religious thought, we are on more uncertain ground. In 7:17 ff., in the person of Solomon, the author tells how God gave him knowledge of the organization of the universe, the heavenly bodies, seasonal changes, the powers of spirits, the thoughts of men, and the properties of roots.[44] He sums this up: "I learned such things

[42] For this emanation see Wisd. Sol. 7:25; Sirach 1:4; 24:3 ff. As we noted in n. 33, the description of the origin of Wisdom in Sirach 24 is given to the heavenly assembly; this accounts for its being a mystery. And, of course, we need posit no Hellenistic background for the concept of Wisdom itself (since it appears in Northwest Semitic sources as early as the seventh century B.C.) nor for the idea of emanation. See W. F. Albright, *From the Stone Age to Christianity* (2nd ed.; New York: Doubleday Anchor, 1957), pp. 366-69.

[43] E.g., in describing the scene at Shittim where the Israelites of the Exodus followed the Moabite women into idolatry (Num. 25:3-5; also Ps. 106 [105]: 28), the LXX uses *etelestē*, "was initiated," and Symmachus uses *myeisthai*. See also the LXX of Hos. 4:14; I Kings 15:12; and Symmachus of I Kings 14:24; II Kings 23:7; Isa. 3:3.

[44] For the tradition of Solomon's power over evil spirits and his botanical knowledge, see Josephus, *Antiquities* 8.2.5 (8.42-49). In Enoch we shall again encounter the power of roots as a mystery.

as are secret [*krypta*] and such as are plain, for Wisdom, the
artificer of all, taught me." We might think that we have no more
here than in Sirach 4:18, where we saw Wisdom as an agent of
God revealing mysteries. But later, in Wisd. Sol. 8:4, we hear that
Wisdom "is the initiate in the knowledge of God, and the selector
of his works." The technical mystery-religion term for female
initiate, *mystis*, is here applied to Wisdom.

Thus, in the last of the biblical books, there is evidence for
familiarity with the mystery religions; yet, on the face of it, only
a familiarity which would be the common possession of Alexandrians
in the period just before Christ.[45] As Bornkamm states: "These
passages display no more than influence [of mystery-cult ideas];
the mysteries here are linked neither with sacramental rites nor
with the Gnostic redemption myth."[46]

2. "Mysteries" in the Pseudepigrapha

Since the original texts of the four works we are about to consider (Enoch, II and III Baruch, IV Ezra) are no longer extant,
we must work through later versions. Here we possess a picture of
Judaism in the centuries just before and during the rise of Christianity, providing us with an insight into popular beliefs often
frowned on by more orthodox circles. Currents of belief other than
Pharisaism had their influence on early Christianity. Consequently,
the noncanonical literature must be taken quite seriously in tracing
the development of NT ideas.

(a) Enoch

Enoch, preserved for us in Ethiopic,[47] is most important for our

[45] The problem of the Jews of Alexandria and the mystery religions is very
difficult. We recommend Lucien Cerfaux, "Influence des Mystères sur le
judaïsme alexandrin avant Philon," *Recueil Lucien Cerfaux* (Louvain,
1954) I, pp. 65-112; this should be accompanied with Lagrange's critical
review of Cerfaux's article in *RB,* 34 (1925), pp. 150-2. Karl Prümm,
"Mystères," in Vigouroux' *Dictionnaire de la Bible, Supplément* (Paris),
6 (1957), fasc. 30, col. 175, also finds some exaggeration in Cerfaux's
article. For Philo's attitude toward the mysteries, see Wolfson's *Philo*
(cited above, n. 41), I, pp. 36-53, which may be contrasted with an opposite
view expressed by E. R. Goodenough in his review of Wolfson in *JBL,*
67 (1948), esp. pp. 91-93.
[46] *TDNT, "mystērion"* (article cited above, n. 1), p. 814.
[47] R. H. Charles has collated 29 mss. in his *Ethiopic Version of the Book
of Enoch* (*Anecdota Oxoniensia,* XI, 1906). The Ethiopic is probably a
translation from Greek. We now have three Greek witnesses: (1) Gᵍ
consisting of fragments of chaps. 1-32 found at Akhmim; (2) Gˢ fragments in George Syncellus, the eighth-century Byzantine chronographer—
both of these are published in Charles; (3) fragments consisting of chaps.
97-104, 106-7, published by Campbell Bonner, *The Last Chapters of Enoch
in Greek* (K. and S. Lake's *Studies and Documents,* VIII, 1937).

topic. The book, originally written in Aramaic,[48] is probably composite in nature[49]; an overall date of *c.* 100 B.C. may be accepted as a working hypothesis, but some of the material used in the book is undoubtedly earlier. There are many different types of heavenly mysteries in Enoch. Although this may be caused in part by the composite nature of the literature, in general the various uses of mystery cut across the traditional divisions of sources.[50] A topical arrangement of the material seems the only feasible process.[51]

(i) *Evil Mysteries*

Chapters 6-11 of Enoch give an expanded version of Genesis 6:1-4—the story of how the sons of God came into the daughters of men. We are told how the angels lusted after women, descended to earth, took wives, and begot giants. The latter wreaked havoc until God sent the good angels to punish them and their parents. One of the chief sins of the angels was the revealing of the heavenly mysteries to their earthly mistresses. The good angels complain to God: "You see what 'Azāz'ēl has done, how he has taught all sorts of iniquity on earth, and has revealed the eternal secrets."[52] The

---

[48] As maintained by C. C. Torrey, "Notes on the Greek Text of Enoch," *Journal of the American Oriental Society*, 62 (1942), pp. 52-60. Fragments of ten Aramaic mss. of Enoch have been discovered at Qumran. Most of them run close to the Ethiopic and Greek; but the mss. of the astronomical treatise (chaps. 72-82) witness a fuller text. Cf. J. T. Milik, *Ten Years of Discovery in the Wilderness of Judaea* (London: SCM, 1958), p. 33.

[49] R. H. Charles, *Apocrypha and Pseudepigrapha of the Old Testament* (Oxford: Clarendon, 1913)—henceforth cited as *AP*—II, pp. 168 ff., claimed to recognize five sections, each capable of subdivision. His section II (chaps. 37-71, the "Parables") has not been represented at Qumran. J. T. Milik (cited above, n. 48), p. 33, claims that the absence of chaps. 37-71 at Qumran indicates that they are the work of a Judeo-Christian of the first or second century A.D. Because we do not regard this as certain, we will not hesitate to cite passages from section II of Enoch. If it should prove to be true that this part of Enoch is late, there is still the problem of sources and pre-Christian substratum.

[50] A notable exception is the absence of mysteries in chaps. 17-36. Charles, *AP*, II, pp. 168-9, says that these chapters are composed of two independent sections: 17-19 and 20-36. We might note that chapters 1-17 mention only evil mysteries.

[51] We have checked our translations of the texts to be given above directly with the Ethiopic; this is important since, as we shall see, Charles occasionally emends the difficult readings. "Mystery" or "secret" is expressed in Ethiopic by *mesṭīr* and *ḥebu'*, both of which can translate *mystērion*, as is seen from the Greek fragments. *Mesṭīr* is probably a loan word from *mystērion*; but the form without the emphatic consonant (*mestīr*), which often appears, was probably connected in popular etymology to *satara*, "to hide" (see n. 23 above).

[52] 9:6-8, *ḥebū'āta 'ālam—mystēria tou aiōnos*. See also 65:11.

nature of these forbidden mysteries is made clear in several lists:[53] charms and enchantments; cutting of roots; information about plants; the art of making swords and armor; the metals of the earth and how to work them; ornaments, cosmetics, and costly stones. In other words, the revelation of the mysteries pertained to materials to be used in the wicked arts of sorcery, idolatry, bloodshed, and seduction—truly practices of which Enoch may say: ". . . by these mysteries men and women have multiplied evil on the earth."[54]

One of the problems of these evil mysteries is the hint that they may have been enacted in heaven before the Watchers descended to earth. The two most important texts unfortunately present textual difficulties. In 16:3 God reproaches the fallen Watchers: "You were in heaven and (all) the secrets had not yet been revealed to you; but *you knew the evil mysteries*, and these you announced to the women in the hardness of your heart."[55] The Greek (G^g) of the italicized passage reads: ". . . but you knew the mystery brought about by God"—a reading which gives God a role in fashioning the evil mysteries. A second text (9:6) reads: "He [the evil angel] revealed the eternal secrets *which were being done* in heaven."[56] Of course, the text can be emended (as Charles does: "which were preserved in heaven"); but, as it stands, this passage and the preceding one suggest some sort of belief that evil mysteries were enacted in heaven before the Watchers introduced them to men.

(ii) *Cosmic Mysteries*

Another class of mysteries deals with the workings of different cosmic elements: stars, sun, moon, lightning, thunder, winds, weather, and the different metals. (The most complete list is 60:11-22.) This is not the same as our use of "mystery" to refer to phenomena—e.g., electricity—which we do not understand; for in Enoch natural phenomena are not considered mysteries in them-

[53] 7:1 ff.; 8:1 ff.; 69:1 ff. For the mysterious power of roots, see n. 44 above. The objection to cosmetics and finery may be connected to Isa. 3:16-24; also Testament of Reuben 5:5-6. As Enoch 65:6 tells us, the knowledge of metals is objectionable because they were used to make idols. 69:9-10 lists as an evil mystery the art of writing; this is an interesting contrast to Jubilees 4:17, where Enoch is praised as the first among men who learned to write.
[54] 16:3: *mestir*. Also 10:7.
[55] The "all" is in the Greek, not the Ethiopic.
[56] 9:6. G^g has a long and seemingly corrupt reading on which Charles, *AP*, II, p. 193, bases his translation.

selves, but only in reference to divine providence. Each of these cosmic mysteries has an ethical or religious value which constitutes part of the secret. Let us illustrate.

In one of his visions of the operation of the world, Enoch says: "And there my eyes saw the secrets [*ḥebū'āta*] of the lightning and of the thunder; and the secrets of the winds . . . and the secrets of the clouds and dew (41:3)." He goes on to describe the paths of the sun and moon as they leave their chambers and follow their orbits. But the lesson is that all is arranged and fulfilled according to God's will (41:6) and that these bodies give light to the just and darkness to sinners. Further on (43:1-4), Enoch tells us: "And I saw other lightnings and the stars of heaven; and I saw how He called them each by its name, and they obeyed Him." And so Enoch asks his angelic guide[57] about the stars and their revolutions; and he is informed of their parabolic meaning: "These are the names of the saints who dwell on earth, and believe in the name of the Lord of spirits for ever and ever."

In 71:4 we hear: "And he showed me all the secrets of righteousness; and he showed me all the secrets of the ends of the heavens, and all the chambers of the stars and all the luminaries." It is not clear what the secrets of righteousness are, nor whether they are in apposition to the secrets that follow; but at any rate we have another mixture of the moral and the cosmic. So sacred is the mystery of the order of the heavenly bodies that it is hidden from sinners; and this is the source of their idolatrous worship of the stars (80:7). One final example of natural mysteries is that of the secrets of the mountains of metals (iron, copper, silver, gold, etc.) in chapter 52. We get not one but two explanations of the metals, probably re-

[57] Throughout these visions the mysteries are explained to Enoch by an angel. Bornkamm, *TDNT*, "*mystērion*" (article cited above, n. 1), p. 816, compares the role of these angels to that of the mystagogues in the mystery religions. Such a comparison has little basis in Ethiopic Enoch, which shows no profound assimilation of Greek ideas. Rather, the role of angels as guides to the heavenly secrets would flow quite naturally from our theory that the heavenly *sôd* was the ultimate background of the revelation of the divine mysteries.

We might note that Enoch speaks of the heavenly mysteries as existing, concrete realities, so that one sees them as if on a guided tour through an unknown land. It is difficult to decide how much of this description is poetic imagery, and how much reality the authors attributed to the hidden mountains, chambers, etc. Even the less tangible events, such as future happenings, are treated as if already existing in heaven. See Bornkamm, *ibid.*, p. 815.

flecting, as Charles maintains,[58] two different sources. For the author of 52:5-9, these mountains of metal are evil, and will be destroyed when the Elect appears. For the author of 52:4, these mountains seem to be good: "All these things which you have seen shall serve the dominion of His messiah that he may command and be strong on earth." In both instances the mysteries are important for their role in God's plan of salvation.

(iii) *Mysteries of God's Will and Human Actions*

By far the most frequent use of mystery in the Enoch literature concerns God's will as it affects mankind. Naturally, nothing of man's fate is a mystery for God himself: "You know and see and hear everything, and there is nothing hidden from you, for you see everything" (84:3). On the other hand, God and his actions constitute the great mystery for mankind. In their hymn of glory to the Lord of spirits, the fallen angels cry out: "And your power will shine forth in every mystery to all generations, and your glory for ever and ever; all your mysteries are deep and numberless."[59] Enoch is one of the fortunate ones to whom the mysteries of God are revealed, including the destiny of man.[60]

It is natural that "mystery" be used to refer to the future of man. Yet, in one interesting case, a thing of the past is called a mystery. In 60:7-10 the creation story is told in terms of Leviathan and Behemoth, two great monsters dwelling in the abyss and the desert. When the angel is asked to show the might of these monsters, and how they were separated, he replies: "In regard to this, O man, you want to know something that is secret." The passage breaks off, and we never get an answer.

The "mysteries," when applied to human actions, cover both evil and good deeds. In chapter 83 Mahalalel, the father of Enoch, remarks concerning his son's dream-vision of the destruction of the earth: "You have seen a thing of grave import, my son; and the vision of your dream is more important than [or important in

---

[58] *AP* II, p. 219. There is some variation in the number of metallic mountains. See 67:4.

[59] 63:3. This is similar to Sirach 11:4.

[60] E.g., 41:1, "And after this I saw all the secrets of the heavens; and how the kingdom is divided; and the deeds of men, how they are weighed on the scale." The kingdom in question may be heaven, or, more likely, the messianic kingdom. The verse is followed by a list of cosmic mysteries which belong to another context (Charles, *AP*, II, p. 212).

reference to] the secrets of all the sins of the earth."[61] For "mysteries" referring to righteous actions, we have a possible instance in 38:3: when the Righteous One shall appear, "the secrets of the just shall be revealed; the sinners shall be judged."[62] A clearer passage is 49:2, where we are told that the Elect One "is mighty in all the secrets of righteousness." The context describes how the Elect One possesses the spirit of wisdom, understanding, etc. When we are informed that the Elect One "shall judge the hidden things" (49:4, 61:9), the term seems to apply collectively to the actions of man, both good and bad. At first it may seem strange that man's deeds can be called mysteries. But the term is applied most frequently in reference to God's judgment, when even man's most hidden thoughts shall be revealed (cf. Sirach 1:30). From the unknown good or bad actions done in private and to be revealed at the end, the connotation of mystery may have spread to other actions.

A logical development is the application of "mystery" to God's judgment itself. In one case (89:1) a temporal judgment on human actions, the Deluge, is called a *mesṭīr*. But the mystery par excellence is the final judgment and its aftermath. In 68:5 Michael says to Raphael that he will not defend the fallen angels, for the Lord has been angry with them: "Wherefore there will happen to them all that is hidden [one ms. reads "the hidden judgment"] for ever and ever." Again, in reference to the impious boast that both the sinners and the just have the same fate after death, Enoch swears that he knows a mystery (*mesṭīr-mystērion*) from reading the heavenly tablets: the righteous shall be rewarded, but the evil punished (103:2). Further, the destiny of people who are dead but who have yet to be judged seems to be called a mystery. In the vision of chapter 61, angels are sent off to the north to get the measures or measurements of the just. When Enoch asks the meaning of this, he is told: "And these measurements shall reveal all the secrets of the depths of the earth, and those who have been destroyed by the desert . . . by the beasts . . . by the fish of the sea, that they may

---

[61] 83:7. Another example of "mysteries" applied to sins may be 68:2, where the angel Michael is provoked "concerning the severity of the judgment [of the bad angels] in reference to (?) the secrets." The passage offers some difficulty, however.

[62] Charles, *AP*, II, p. 209, however, takes this to mean that the secret rewards in store for the just shall be revealed; he cites 58:5, "And after this it will be said to the saints in heaven that they should seek out the secrets of righteousness, the heritage of faith; for it has become bright as the sun upon earth and the darkness has passed." But even here it is not clear whether the "secrets of righteousness" are rewards or good actions.

return and support themselves on the day of the Elect One. For none shall be destroyed before the Lord of spirits."

The last stage in the connection of mystery to judgment is the application of the term to the Elect One, the Son of Man who shall be the judge. We hear that the Son of Man (so named before creation), the staff of righteousness, and the light of the nations, "was chosen and *hidden* in His presence before the world was yet made until eternity."[63] But on the day of judgment God shall reveal the hidden Son of Man to the elect (48:7; 62:1). He has been guarding the future inheritance of the elect, and now he shall judge them. "His mouth shall pour forth all the secrets of wisdom and counsel, for the Lord of spirits has given (them) to him and glorified him" (51:3, 62:2). There will then ensue the days of blessedness for the just, and punishment for the wicked. The Son of Man may be referred to, also, in the enigmatic passage about the secret name. The angel who keeps the heavenly oath requests Michael "that he reveal to them [the angels] the hidden name in order that they might mention it in the oath, so that they who revealed all the secrets to mankind might tremble before that name and oath" (69:14).

This concludes our list of the mysteries spoken of in Enoch. Comparing them to the mysteries encountered in the OT, we find that the evil mysteries revealed by the fallen angels are a new facet, yet one quite consonant with the notion of the heavenly assembly—only, here the information is brought out illegitimately. As for cosmic phenomena, they were mysteries in Sirach too (43:32; 16:21); but the idea is more fully treated in Enoch. Sirach again has in embryo the application of "mysteries" to human actions and God's judgment of them. Here Enoch not only develops the use of the term, but applies it to the hidden person who will be the instrument of judgment. Whereas Sirach stressed that secrets could be learned from the law, the wisdom books, and the prophets, Enoch, in harmony with its extracanonical status, purports to be a collection of mysteries handed down by a mysterious personage to his descendants.[64] Consequently, while in some usages of "mystery" Enoch

[63] 48:6. Also 62:7, "From the beginning the Son of Man was hidden, and the Most High kept him in the presence of His might; and revealed him to the elect."
[64] 68:1. A relative of Enoch tells us that Enoch handed over to him the teaching of all the mysteries in a book, together with the parables. In chapter 104 Enoch himself solemnly announces two last mysteries, the second of which is that his own words, faithfully written down, will be a cause of joy to the righteous.

comes close to Sirach, the two are very far apart in the manner and spirit of revelation. In this aspect Enoch is closer to Daniel and the apocalyptic literature.

(b) *Baruch Literature*

Just as a literature attached itself to the enigmatic figure of Enoch, so, somewhat later, in the last era of the Second Temple, the figure of Baruch became the vehicle of a group of apocalypses.[65] The hard times that had fallen on Judea recalled to mind the secretary of Jeremiah who, along with his master, had withstood the collapse of the first Israelite commonwealth; and on his lips were placed consoling words for those who were witnesses of a second destruction of Jerusalem. At first, this literature might seem too late to be included in a discussion of the pre-Christian Semitic background of *mystērion*. However, at least in the case of II Baruch (on which we shall concentrate) we have a Jewish work roughly contemporary with Paul's last years, and therefore useful as a witness to the last development of the concept that is independent of Christianity.[66] Moreover, the origins of the pseudepigraphical Baruch literature are older than formerly conceded. At Qumran, there are fragments of about six manuscripts of a pseudo-Jeremianic literature which have points of contact with our Baruch texts.[67]

II Baruch describes the visions accorded to Baruch amid the ruins of Jerusalem after the city had fallen to Nebuchadnezzar. Throughout, Baruch asks God for an interpretation of these strange visions (which are reminiscent of the NT Apocrypha), and on occasion he uses the term "mysteries."

---

[65] We are interested in II Baruch or the Syriac Apocalypse of Baruch, and III Baruch or the Greek Apocalypse. We have used the one complete Syriac text of II Baruch published by Ceriani, *Monumenta Sacra et Profana* (1871) V, 2, pp. 113-80. The Syriac is probably a translation of a Greek translation made from a lost Hebrew (?) original. We have used the Greek text of III Baruch published by M. R. James in Cambridge *Texts and Studies*, V, 1 (*Apocrypha Anecdota*, iii, 1897).

[66] R. H. Charles, *The Apocalypse of Baruch* (2nd ed.; London: Black, 1896), p. xvi, dates the composition between A.D. 50-90, with final redaction slightly later (p. lxv). Bruno Violet, *Die Apokalypsen des Ezra und des Baruchs* ("Die griechischen christlichen Schriftsteller"; Leipzig, 1924), II, p. xci, dates the book *c.* A.D. 100-120. For the purely Jewish origins of II Baruch, see Charles, *AP*, II, p. 470.

[67] J. Strugnell, *RB*, 63 (1956), p. 65.

The Semitic Background of "Mystery"

(i) Cosmic Mysteries

In his prayer in 48:2-3, Baruch says to God: "You give order to the ways of the seasons and they are obedient to you. You alone know the duration of generations; and you do not reveal your mysteries [r'zyk] to many." The surrounding verses seem to identify these mysteries: the seasons, duration of generations, fire, wind, darkness. We hear an echo of the same idea in 54:1, "You alone, O Lord, know aforetime the profound things of the world; and you bring about by your word the things which befall in their times. . . . And the end of seasons you alone know." We do not wish to treat III Baruch in detail, since the book seems to show signs of Christian redaction.[68] We would mention here only that it develops the cosmic mysteries at length. Baruch is taken on a tour through the seven heavens by an angel who promises to show him the "mysteries of God" (III Baruch 1:8). Some of the mysteries are purely physical: the measurements of the heavenly plains, the chariot of the sun, the source of the rains, etc. But in these celestial mysteries there are also strong spiritual overtones. In the heavenly plains, e.g., there are present the builders of the tower of Babel (chap. 3), the dragon of evil, the tree of Adam's sin (chap. 4). Thus the ideas of the Enoch literature had a continuation even after the end of the Second Commonwealth.

(ii) Mysteries of the Last Times

In his epistle (II Baruch 76-86), Baruch consoles the Israelites in the Babylonian captivity. He thanks God that "He has made known to me the mystery (mysteries) of the times, and the advent of the hours He showed me."[69] From the context, he seems to mean the ultimate destruction of evil at the end of the world, when God comes to judge. Another indication of this is 85:8 ff.: "Again, moreover, the Most High . . . has shown us what is to come, and has not hidden from us anything which will come to pass in the end. . . . The coming of the times is almost here."

---

[68] Hughes, *AP*, II, p. 529. There is no real evidence that III Baruch (second century A.D.) is closely connected to II Baruch.

[69] 81:4. The mss. vary in pointing r'z' dzbn' as singular or plural.

(c) *IV Ezra*

Ezra[70] is another figure who, at the end of the Second Common-wealth, became the vehicle of pseudo-prophecies referring to the fall and rise of Jerusalem. His visions (patterned after those of Daniel), which promise the ultimate consolation of Israel and the destruction of her enemies, are again set ·in the period after the capture of Jerusalem in 587—thirty years after the fall, according to IV Ezra 3:1.

Throughout the work[71] we see that because of his excellent life Ezra received a revelation of the mysteries of God, i.e., the future that God has in store for Jerusalem and the world (see 6:32-3). In 10:38 the angel Uriel tells Ezra: "Hear me and I shall inform you and tell you concerning the things which you fear: for the Most High has revealed many mysteries to you, for he has seen that your way is right."[72] And then Uriel proceeds to explain how the vision of the suffering woman which Ezra has seen refers to Zion, who will shine forth in glory again. In 14:5 Ezra is told that he is not the only one who has seen the "secrets of the times," for on Mt. Sinai God told Moses many wondrous things ". . . and showed him the secrets of the times, and (declared to him) the end of the times."[73]

Not all of Ezra's visions are to be made public. Only part (twenty-four books—presumably the canonical OT) is to be trans-mitted to Ezra's contemporaries in the Babylonian exile; the rest (seventy books—pseudepigraphical literature) is to be written down and given to the wise among the people who will preserve it (14:26, 44). This is an interesting attempt to make the apocryphal literature

[70] It is disputed whether or not the Ezra of IV Ezra (also called II Esdras) is the prophet Ezra of the late fifth century. See W. O. E. Oesterley, *II Esdras* (Westminster Commentaries, 1933), pp. xii-xv. This Ezra apocalypse is probably to be dated to the beginning of the second century A.D. See Oesterley, p. xliv, and Violet (cited n. 66, above), II, p. xlix.

[71] Generally thought to have been written in Hebrew, IV Ezra is preserved only in versions presumably translated from Greek. For the Latin (the most important version) we cite from Violet's critical text. This should be compared to the Syriac in Ceriani (cited above, n. 65), V, 1 (1868), pp. 41-111; and to the Ethiopic in Dillmann, *Veteris Testamenti Aethiopici*, V (1894), pp. 153-93.

J. Bloch, "The Ezra-Apocalypse: Was it Written in Hebrew, Greek or Aramaic?" *Jewish Quarterly Review*, 48 (1958), pp. 293-94, denies that Greek was the basis of the versions, and suggests that Aramaic was the original language.

[72] Latin *mysteria multa* and Syriac *r'z' sgy'* (Ethiopic "hidden mystery" *meṣṭîr ḥebū'*). Violet (cited above, n. 66) II, 144, translates as "great mysteries," suggesting that the original may have been *sôdîm rabbîm*.

[73] Latin has "secret times" (*tempora secreta*); but the Syriac *r'z' dzbn'* and the Ethiopic *meṣṭîra mawā'el* favor our translation.

as authentic a heritage as the canonical books. Of course, the "mysteries" of God come under the injunction of secrecy. In 12:36-37 Ezra is told: "You alone have been found worthy to learn this mystery [*secretum*; variant, *sacramentum*] of the Most High. Therefore write all these things that you have seen in a book and put them in a secret place. And you shall teach them to the wise among your people whose hearts you know can comprehend and keep these mysteries." A similar injunction was laid upon Moses when the mysteries were revealed to him (14:6).

Thus what we see in IV Ezra is really only one type of mystery: the symbolic vision concerned with the last times and the destiny of Israel. And so, while the cosmic mysteries of the Baruch literature lie close to Enoch, IV Ezra is more directly in the heritage of Daniel.

3. "MYSTERIES" IN THE QUMRAN LITERATURE

The sectarian literature which we shall now treat can be dated to about the first century B.C.,[74] coming after most of the OT deuterocanonical books (except Wisdom of Solomon), perhaps shortly after parts of Enoch, and before the NT, II Baruch, and IV Ezra. The idea of "mysteries" plays an important role within this body of literature.[75]

(i) *Mysteries of Divine Providence*

The first type of mystery that we might distinguish at Qumran concerns God's providence as it affects angels, men, and the future of Israel. For an example dealing with the angels, we hear this praise of God: ". . . for great is your majestic plan and your marvelous mysteries [*rzy nplwtykh*] on high with you for raising up to you from the dust, and casting down the angels."[76] The text

---

[74] See W. F. Albright, "Recent Discoveries in Bible Lands," a supplement to Young's *Analytical Concordance to the Bible* (22nd ed.; New York: Funk & Wagnalls, 1955), p. 50; and F. M. Cross, Jr., *The Ancient Library of Qumran* (New York: Doubleday, 1958), pp. 89 ff. The date is approximate: some of the present *copies* are first century A.D., while, on the other hand, the composition of some of the works goes back to the second century B.C. (e.g., Cross dates the composition of 1QS before 100 B.C.). For CD, although we depend on a medieval copy, one of the Qumran mss. is preRoman; and Cross dates the composition of the work to *c*. 100 B.C. (p. 59, n. 46).

[75] For a convenient list of passages, see E. Vogt, " 'Mysteria' in textibus Qumran," *Biblica*, 37 (1956), pp. 247-57. *Rāz* is the most frequent term; but *sôd* occurs often, at times in parallelism with *rāz*, or interchanged for it in set expressions. *Nistārôt* also appears.

[76] 1QM 14:14. The 1QM text has lacunae which must be filled in from 4QM^a—see C.-H. Hunzinger, "Fragmente einer ältern Fassung des Buches *Milḥama*," *Zeitschrift für die Alttestamentliche Wissenschaft*, 69, (1957), p. 141.

is not clear, but it is evident that God's mysterious plan affects even the angels. 1QS 3:20-23 tells us that all evil persons are under the dominion of the angel of darkness, and even the righteous err through him "according to the mysteries of God [*rzy 'l*] until the final time set by him." But in "the mysteries of his intelligence [*brzy śklw*]" and his glorious wisdom, God has appointed an end for the existence of evil (1QS 4:18).

For the mysterious dispositions of God in reference to men, we hear the psalmist's assurance that God will help his cause: "For (although) you have chastised me in the mystery of your wisdom [*brz ḥkmtkh*], and hidden the truth until . . . in the appointed time, then your chastisement will be joy and gladness to me."[77] The break in the text may refer to a future revelation of God's plan which will enable the writer to understand his chastisement. In the War we see God's mysterious providence in his selection of those who are to fall: ". . . the slain among (our) soldiers begin to fall by the mysteries of God to test thereby all those who are eager for the war."[78] Following up this idea, the high priest exhorts the soldiers: "And you, children of this covenant, be strong in the trial from God until he waves his hand and completes the trials: his mysteries are for your support."[79] A similar aspect of providence may be hinted at in 1QH Frag. 3:7, where we find God keeping someone or something "according to the mysteries of his good pleasure [*lrzy ḥpṣw*]."

The best example for "mystery" used of the future of Israel is the commentary on Habakkuk 2:1-2 ("Write the vision and make it plain (?) on tablets, that he who runs may read it"):

And God told Habakkuk to write down what was to come upon the latter age, but the fulfillment of the end [*gml hqṣ*] He did not reveal

[77] 1QH 9:23-4. We have translated the hiphil of *ykḥ* as "chastised"; Vogt (cited above, n. 75), p. 255, renders it as "instruxisti."
[78] 1QM 16:11: *brzy 'l*. See also 16:15-16: "Blessed be God who strengthens the heart of his people, (who) tests by ———— your slain, because from of old you have heard of the mysteries of God."
[79] 1QM 17:8-9. The cryptic *rzyw lm'mdkh* is difficult. In Ps. 69:3 *m'md* is a place to stand on in rising waters; in Mishnaic Hebrew *m'myd* is "support." In the War Scroll it is a term of military organization (Y. Yadin, *The Scroll of the War of the Sons of Light Against the Sons of Darkness* [Oxford, 1962], p. 146) but here it may refer to the role given to man by God (so Yadin, p. 341, note; he translates: "until he shall lift up his hand and shall complete his testings through his *mysteries with regard to your existence*"). J. Strugnell, *CBQ*, 29 (1967), p. 582, suggests that *rzyw* is a misreading and that the passage does not pertain to "mysteries."

to him. And the interpretation of his saying 'that he who runs may read it' refers to the Teacher of Righteousness to whom God has revealed *all the secrets of the words of his servants the prophets.*[80]

Thus the future of Israel was hidden in prophecies; but, that one might read it, it was necessary that God reveal the secrets of these prophecies. The commentator goes on to tell us that the coming of the end has been delayed beyond all prophetic expectation, "for the mysteries of God are to be marvelous" (1QpHab. 7:8). All things are to come in due time "as He has ordained for them in the mysteries of his wisdom [*brzy 'rmtw*]" (7:13-14). A final example of "mystery" applied to God's plan for the future is found in 1QS 11:3-4, "From the well of his knowledge he has enlightened me; and made my eye contemplate his wonders; and the light of my heart, the mystery to be [*rz nhyh*]."

(ii) *Mysteries of the Sect's Interpretation of the Law*

In Qumran theology one of the marvelous mysteries of God is the peculiar interpretation of the law he has entrusted to the community:

From the source of his righteousness are my judgments;
From his marvelous mysteries [*rzy pl'w*] is there a light in my heart.
My eye has contemplated what is eternal;
Sound wisdom which is hidden [*nstrh*] from wise men,
    and discretion (hidden) from mankind. . .
A fountain of glory (hidden) from the worldly assembly—
God has granted these to those whom he elected as an eternal possession.
He has constituted them as an inheritance in the lot of the saints;
And he has joined their society [*swdm*] with the sons of heaven into a
    unified congregation and an assembly [*swd*] of saintly fabric.[81]

The author, then, has seen marvelous mysteries hidden from ordinary men, mysteries and wisdom which are the inheritance of the Qumran community.

The background of this special knowledge is found in CD. Here, after speaking of the rebellious Israelites who forsook God's covenant in the wilderness, the writer tells us that with those who kept his commands God established an eternal covenant "by revealing

---

[80] 1QpHab. 7:1-ɔ: *kwl rzy dbry 'bdyw hnb'ym*—undoubtedly a reminiscence of Amos 3:7, where God reveals his *sôd* to his servants the prophets.
[81] 1QS 11:5-8. The last line is an echo which connects the community's special knowledge of divine mysteries with the ancient notion of the angelic *sôd*.

to them the hidden things [*nstrwt*] in which all Israel had gone astray" (3:12-14). These hidden things consisted of his holy sabbaths, his glorious feasts, ordinances, ways of truth, and the purposes of his will. When men continued to sin even after this revelation, once again "God in his marvelous mysteries [*rzy pl'w*, i.e., his providence] forgave their iniquity and pardoned their sin. And he built for them a firm house in Israel, the like of which had never stood until now" (3:18-20). Thus the Qumran community by a process of historical selection became God's final repository of the hidden commands, the observance of which is necessary for life.

Any who wish to join are "to act according to the interpretation of the Torah in which their forefathers had been instructed."[82] One of the prime responsibilities of those instructed in the "secret counsels of the spirit [*swdy rwḥ*] for the sons of truth in the world" (1QS 4:6), is to keep the mysteries of knowledge (*rzy d't*) hidden from outsiders, or even from untrained initiates.[83] But the full-fledged members of the community are to be taught the truth "to guide them in knowledge and so to make them wise in the marvelous and true mysteries amidst the men of the community" (1QS 9:18-19).[84]

The writer (or writers) of the *Hôdāyôt* seems to have had a special role in such instruction. Amidst his persecution, he can still say, "You have set me up as a banner for the righteous elect, as the interpreter of knowledge in your marvelous mysteries, to test [the men or seekers] of truth, and to try the lovers of discipline" (2:13-14). In another psalm he says that through him God has illuminated many: "For you have instructed me in your marvelous mysteries [*rzy pl'kh*] and by your wonderful secret counsel [*swd pl'kh*] you have shown your power toward me" (4:27-28). The question of the betrayal of this secret knowledge arises; for the psalmist says that those who had been intimates in his secret counsel (*nṣmdy swdy*) now "go to the sons of perdition bearing false tales

---

[82] CD 4:8. In 5:2-4 there is a cryptic reference to the book of the law sealed in the ark and not opened till Zadok arose. The Qumranians seemingly considered this hidden book the ancestor of their own tradition.

[83] 1QS 4:6. For other commands of secrecy see 9:17 and 22; and CD 15:10-11. All this is consonant with Josephus' information about Essene secrecy (*Jewish War* 2.8.7 [2.137-42]).

[84] J. Licht, *Israel Exploration Journal,* 8 (1958), p. 111, gives good evidence for an interesting rearrangement of this text: "And also to instruct them in the mysteries of wonder and truth; to walk perfectly, one with the other, among the men of the community, in all that is revealed in them."

The Semitic Background of "Mystery"

about the mystery which you have concealed in me . . . and because of their sin you have concealed the fount of wisdom and the secret (source?) of truth."[85]

In connection with this secret knowledge of the community, we may mention the blind unwillingness on the part of outsiders to obtain it. 1QS 5:11 says of the men of error, "These are not counted in his covenant, for they have not sought nor studied God's statutes for the knowledge of the hidden things (*nstrwt*) in which they erred."[86] The 1QH Frag. 6:5 has the words: "You have not revealed your mysteries [*rzykh*]"—perhaps to the wilfully blind.

The hymn of 1QH 8:4-36 is very important for the mysteries of the Qumrân interpretation of the law. However, it is an exceedingly difficult allegory based on the first chapters of Genesis and on Psalm 1; we shall sketch our interpretation without taking time to justify our readings.[87] At a source of water (the law), God planted many trees (the Israelites) for his glorification. A special group were the "trees of life at a secret fount," concealed among the other trees. These seem to be the elect ones among the Israelites who draw upon the correct interpretation of the Law. The trees of life put forth a "branch for an eternal planting" (the Qumran community—cf. CD 1:7); and since these trees have access to living water, the branch develops into a large tree. The branch is attacked by the other trees (the persecution of the Qumran group), but in some way the holy branch is hidden and its mystery (*rzw*) sealed off. In particular God is said to have fenced off the fruit of the branch (Teacher of Righteousness? cf. CD 1:11) "with the mystery of the mighty in strength [*brz gbwry kwḥ*] and holy spirits." In 1QH 5:11-12 we have an example of the fence that hides the fruit or Teacher, for it is said that God hid the author from men until the time when He would reveal to him His salvation. Here the

85 1QH 5:25-26, *strt m'yn bynh wswd 'mt*. The expression *sôd 'ĕmet* occurs frequently. In 1QH 1:26-27; 10:4-5; 11:4, "secret of truth" or "counsel of truth" is an adequate translation. But in the passage at hand, as well as 1QH 2:9-10 and 5:8-9, the expression seems to mean a "(secret?) source of truth." A. Dupont-Sommer, *Le Livre des Hymnes découvert près de la Mer Morte* (*Semitica* VII; Paris: Maisonneuve, 1957), p. 29, n. 2, translates it as "foundation," perhaps connecting it to the root *ysd*.
86 The *nistārôt* evokes the "hidden sins" of Ps. 19:13, but here it seems to be a question of culpable ignorance. See F. Nötscher, *Zur theologischen Terminologie der Qumran-Texte* (Bonn: Hanstein, 1956), p. 71.
87 For other interpretations differing in certain details, see Dupont-Sommer (cited above, n. 85), pp. 62 ff., and Vogt (cited above, n. 75), p. 254. also Meir Wallenstein, *The Nezer and the Submission in Suffering Hymn from the Dead Sea Scrolls* (Istanbul: Nederlands Instituut, 1957).

fence consists in part of the valiant angelic powers of the community; we may compare this to 1Q36:16, where we hear of "men in custody of your mysteries ['*nšy mšmrt lrzykh*]." The allegory concludes with the theme of community victory. Despite the intricacy of the figures involved, we can see the important uses of mystery in this passage. Not only is the law a secret source of life entrusted to the group; but also, if we are correct, a person is spoken of as hidden. This is reminiscent of the Enoch literature where the Elect One is hidden until judgment.[88]

(iii) *Cosmic Mysteries*

The *Hôdāyôt* open with a psalm of praise for God, who assigned roles for all creation and allotted the eternal spirits their domain. Understanding a phrase like "You did give an assignment," we read: ". . . to the luminaries for their secrets, to the stars for their paths, ... for their burdens."[89] Here the secrets are the orbits of the heavenly bodies, which are beyond the author's understanding. The psalmist goes on describing meteors, lightnings, waters, earth, man's spirit and its destiny. Referring to all these, he tells us: "These things I have known through your intelligence, for you have opened my ears to your marvelous mysteries."[90] In another place the psalmist speaks of how he will praise God at all times: in the day, which attends the fixed course of the sun; in the night; at the moments when the seasons begin—all of which are determined by divine decree. "And I, endowed with wisdom, have known you, O my God, through the spirit which you have given me; and I have heard what is certain in your marvelous mysteries [*swd pl'kh* for the usual *rz pl'*] through your holy spirit. You have opened up within me

---

[88] While working in the Jerusalem scrollery, preparing a concordance of the unpublished Qumran cave 4 material, the writer came across a phrase which expresses exactly the mysteries of the Qumran interpretation of the law: *n]stry twrtk*—the mysteries of your law (from 4QSl.11*b* 2,2—quoted with the kind permission of Prof. John Strugnell).

[89] 1QH 1:11-12, *m'wrwt lrzyhm*. In line 13 we have again: ———— *lrzyhm*. Vogt (cited above, n. 75), pp. 252-53, suggests that part of the mystery may be that these orbits help to determine the sacred times of the Qumran feasts.

[90] 1QH 1:21. Parenthetically we note that in lines 27-30 this hymn applies the term "mysteries" to the paths of human speech: "You made the sounds go forth according to their secrets, and the utterances of breath according to their plans." For the translation, and the possibility that the text refers to poetry and music, see Dupont-Sommer (cited above, n. 85), p. 29, n. 5.

knowledge in the mystery of your wisdom [*brz śklkh*]."[91] The psalmist acknowledges that he has not earned such marvelous wisdom; for no man is righteous with God and no one can understand all his mysteries (1QH 12:19-20; 7:26-32). And, in particular, the worldly man is incapable of understanding divine mysteries: "And in the mysteries of your wisdom you have divi[ded?] all these things to make your glory known; [and unable is] the carnal spirit to understand all these things" (1QH 13:13-14).[92]

(iv) *Evil Mysteries*

While God has given Belial dominion for a time, 1QS 4:1 tells us that God hates the counsel (*sôd*) of this evil spirit. In the War Scroll, a hymn to the faithful God of Israel has these words: ". . . against the dominion of Belial and against his hostile mysteries."[93] What such mysteries might be is not clear; probably they are some sort of hidden evil working in the world. In 1QH 5:36 the psalmist says that even his bread and drink disturb him: ". . . according to the iniquitous mysteries [*kryz pš'*]they deform the works of God in their guilt." Again the exact meaning is not clear.

We hear more of the mysteries of iniquity in the so-called Book of Mysteries (1Q27). In 1:2, surrounded by hopelessly broken context, the words *rzy pš'* appear. Lines 3-4 read: "And they have not known the mystery to come [*rz nhyh*] and have not considered the past; nor have they known what will come on them. And they have not saved their souls from the mystery to come." Isaac Rabinowitz says, "This 'mystery' . . . is the expected consummation in which the idolatrous . . . should be destroyed forever, while Israel's righteous remnant should enjoy eternal dominion."[94] The text goes on to describe the signs of the mystery to come: the evil will disappear

[91] 1QH 12:11-13. The exact connotation of "spirit" is difficult. It could be the good spirit who rules over human actions, or it may be a vague reference to the power of God. See the role of the spirit in Sirach 48:24-25.

[92] Contrast this to 1QH 11:9-10: "Your mercies are unto all the children of your good pleasure; for you have given them knowledge in the mystery of your truth (*swd 'mtkh*), and have given them insight into your marvelous mysteries (*rzy pl'kh*)"—notice the parallelism between *rāz* and *sôd*. See also 1QS 11:15 ff.

[93] 1QM 14:9: *rzy štmtw*. Nötscher (cited above, n. 86), p. 75, finds no clear meaning for these evil mysteries, but makes this suggestion: "Evidently what is meant here is that one does not, or does not rightly, see through the power, essence, and activity of evil, through which man can be brought low."

[94] "The Authorship, Audience and Date of the de Vaux Fragment," *JBL*, 71 (1952), p. 23; there is also a treatise on the translation of *rāz nihyeh* in this article.

like smoke, and justice will appear like the sun.[95] How this will come about we see in the War; for the armies of light, destined to be victorious, march out to battle. On their trumpets for giving the signal for ambush are written the words with which we conclude our survey of Qumran mystery passages: "The mysteries of God for the destruction of evil."[96]

In evaluating the Qumran use of "mystery," we must remember that we have only part of the community's literature,[97] and therefore may have a distorted picture. The cosmic mysteries are present, but without any frequency; in this respect Qumran lies closer to Sirach and the biblical books than to the elaborate development of these mysteries in Enoch and III Baruch. The evil mysteries mentioned at Qumran appear also in Enoch, but there is no evidence the two are the same. At Qumran they seem to be the workings of the spirit who leads the forces of evil against the good—in other words, an aspect of the modified dualistic theology which dominates Qumran thought. In the community's own literature, there is nothing like Enoch's legendary development of the mysteries revealed by the fallen angels, although the presence of copies of Enoch at Qumran may indicate that there was no aversion to such ideas.

As for the Qumran mysteries of divine providence, we have seen this in Enoch and IV Ezra also, but with far more emphasis on

95 In 1:7 there is a very difficult line: _wkwl twmky rzy pl' 'ynmh 'wd._ J. T. Milik, _Discoveries in the Judaean Desert: Qumran Cave I_ (Oxford: Clarendon Press, 1955), p. 103, translates, "And all those who hold back the marvellous mysteries will be no more." Yet _tmk_ more often means "hold on to" than "hold back"; and Vogt (cited above, n. 75), p. 251, n. 7, suggests reading "those who hold on to the mysteries of iniquity," thus _rzy pš'_ rather than _rzy pl'_. The scribe wrote _pl'_ (Milik checked this at my request) but may have made an error; _rzy pš'_ occurs elsewhere in this fragment, as well as in 1QH 5:36 and Frag. 50:5. As J. A. Fitzmyer, _Theological Studies_, 19 (1958), p. 227, has pointed out, we have the Aramaic equivalent of _rz pš'_ in the _rz rš"_ of the Gen. Apoc. 1:2.

96 IQM 3:8-9. T. Gaster, _The Dead Sea Scriptures_ (New York: Anchor, 1956), p. 316, suggests that the ambush gave rise to the use of mysteries on this particular trumpet.

97 E.g., Milik reports that there are several other mss. of the "Book of Mysteries" in cave 4; and Starcky has an eschatological composition which uses _rz_ very frequently—_RB_, 63 (1956), pp. 61, 66. In some _pešer_ literature published by J. M. Allegro in _The Annual of Leeds University Oriental Society_, 4 (1962-63), p. 4, there are several references to _sôd_ in Document II, fragment 1. For instance, line 2 speaks of the rebellion of the wicked from "the council [_sôd_] of the sons of heaven and earth"—perhaps a confirmation that the council of Qumran with its special knowledge of the Torah was thought of as coexisting with the heavenly _sôd_ of the angels.

judgment. Both Qumran and Sirach see the mysteries of God hidden in the writings of old, although Qumran stresses prophecies like Habakkuk while Sirach emphasizes wisdom sayings. As for the manner of knowing the divine mysteries, Qumran, like Sirach, speaks simply of divine revelation without the elaborate visions of Daniel, Enoch, IV Ezra, and III Baruch. There is no mention of Wisdom as a personified agent of revelation at Qumran, only of the holy spirit (again this seems consonant with Qumran's dualism). Finally, in the mysteries of the special interpretation of the Torah, Qumran stands alone in the pre-Christian literature: this concept is part of its sectarian heritage.

We have sought to show that in certain sections of pre-Christian Judaism the notion of divine mysteries was very common. The variety of material subsumed under the idea of "mystery" should warn us that in the NT we may expect a certain variation in the use of the term also.

II

THE SEMITIC BACKGROUND OF
THE NEW TESTAMENT *MYSTĒRION*

THE concept of *mystērion* in the NT has received a great deal of attention,[98] particularly from the viewpoint of its possible relation to the Greek mystery religions. Many have pointed out that there is little real similarity between the Christian mystery and the pagan mysteries,[99] but here we are concerned with the possibility of

[98] Among the best treatments (besides those of Deden and Bornkamm already mentioned in n. 1) are J. A. Robinson, *St. Paul's Epistle to the Ephesians* (cited above, n. 27); K. Prümm, " '*Mystērion*' von Paulus bis Origenes," *Zeitschrift für Katholische Theologie*, 61 (1937), pp. 391-425, and "Zur Phänomenologie des paulinischen *Mystērion*," *Biblica* 37 (1956), pp. 135-61.

[99] The claims of men like Reitzenstein and Bousset have been answered in two ways. First, the limitations of our knowledge of the mystery religions have been carefully presented, e.g., M.-J. Lagrange's treatments of the Eleusinian and Attis mysteries in *RB*, 16 (1919), pp. 157-217 and 419-80; O. Kern and Th. Hopner, "Mysterien," Pauly-Wissowa, *Real-Encyclopädie der klassischen Altertumswissenschaft*, 16² (1935), cols. 1209-1350; K. Prümm, "Mystères" (cited above, n. 45), fasc. 30, cols. 10-225. Second, there have been text-by-text discussions of mystery religion "similarities," e.g., H. A. A. Kennedy, *St. Paul and the Mystery Religions* (London: Hodder and Stoughton, 1913). A good general analysis is H. Rahner's, "The Christian Mystery and the Pagan Mysteries," reprinted in *The Mysteries* (papers from the *Eranos Yearbooks*, 2; New York: Pantheon, 1955), pp. 337-404. A negative answer on the question of mystery-religions influence on Romans 6 is given by G. Wagner in *Pauline Baptism and the Pagan Mysteries* (Edinburgh: Oliver & Boyd, 1967).

a Semitic background for the NT *mystērion*.[100] We plan to study each of the NT passages dealing with *mystērion*, and to point out parallels of thought and vocabulary in the Semitic material studied in the previous chapter. (Naturally we recognize that in some of the postexilic Hebrew literature there was already Hellenistic influence, so that the background is not purely Semitic.) Our purpose is to show that the NT writers, particularly Paul, had in this background all the raw material they needed for the use of "mystery" without venturing into the pagan religions.

1. THE SYNOPTIC PASSAGE

The only occurrence of *mystērion* in the Gospels is a passage in the Synoptics (Matt. 13:10-15; Mark 4:10-12; Luke 8:9-10). Jesus has just narrated the parable of the Sower and the different types of soil on which the seed falls:

Matt. 13	Mark 4	Luke 8
(10) And the disciples came up and said to him, "Why do you speak to them in parables?"	(10) . . . his companions, along with the twelve, asked him about the parables.	(9) But his disciples then began to ask him what this parable meant.
(11) And he answered and said: "To you it is granted to know *the mysteries of the kingdom of the heavens*; but to those it is not granted.	(11) And he said to them: "To you is granted *the mystery of the kingdom of God*; but to those who are outside, everything is in parables;	(10) And he said: "To you it is granted to know *the mysteries of the kingdom of God*; but to the rest in parables;
(13) Wherefore I speak to them in parables because (*hoti*), although looking, they do not see; and although listening, they do not hear nor understand."	(12) in order that (*hina*) although looking, they may see and yet not have perceived; and although listening, they may hear and yet not understand, lest perhaps they should be converted and forgiven."	in order that (*hina*), although looking, they may not see; and although hearing, they may not understand."

[100] Recent articles on this theme include B. Rigaux, "Révélation des mystères et perfection à Qumrân et dans le Nouveau Testament," *NTS*, 4 (1957-58), pp. 237-62; and J. Coppens, "Le 'mystère' dans la théologie paulinienne et ses parallèles qumrâniens," in *Littérature et théologie pauliniennes* ("Recherches bibliques," 5 [1960]), pp. 142-65.

A series of critical problems is raised by this pericope: Was this logion originally spoken by Jesus? Is this logion in its original context?[101] For present purposes, we feel it is better to avoid reconstructions; whether original or not, this logion and its use of *mystērion* has a meaning in its present context, or it would not have been placed there. If we explain it as it stands, we are certain we are explaining a definite NT meaning of *mystērion*; any reconstruction can have the value only of a conjecture.

The question of variants among the three texts also arises.[102] Matthew's "kingdom of heaven" for the "kingdom of God" is a well-known verbal peculiarity. More interesting is the question of Mark's singular *mystērion* vs. the plural of Matthew and Luke. Cerfaux suggests that the plural is more original for two reasons: (*a*) Mark may have been influenced by Paul's predominantly singular usage; (*b*) the frequency of *rāz* as a plural in the Qumran literature, which is a witness of contemporary usage.[103] There is an objection, however, to the second argument: besides *rāz*, Qumran also attests the singular *sôd* for mystery.[104]

Turning from text criticism, we may ask what is meant by the "mystery(ies) of the kingdom of God." The context of the parable of the Sower implies that the kingdom of God is already exercising

[101] C. H. Dodd, *The Parables of the Kingdom* (rev. ed.; New York: Scribner's, 1961), p. 3, regards the logion as a creation of the primitive church to explain the failure to convert the Jews. L. Cerfaux, "La connaissance des secrets du Royaume," *NTS*, 2 (1956), pp. 238-49; and J. Jeremias, *The Parables of Jesus* (rev. ed.; New York: Scribner's, 1963), pp. 14 ff., regard the logion as authentic, although perhaps not in its original context. So also E. Siegman, "Teaching in Parables," *CBQ*, 23 (1961), pp. 161-81; he argues furthermore that the logion is composite and that the prophetic warning that now terminates the logion was originally independent.

[102] Cerfaux (cited above, n. 101) and M.-J. Lagrange, *Évangile selon Saint Matthieu* (8th ed.; Paris: Gabalda, 1948), p. 258, feel that Matthew and Luke have the more authentic tradition. V. Taylor, *The Gospel According to St. Mark* (London: Macmillan, 1953), p. 255, says Mark is more original.

[103] Cerfaux (cited above, n. 101), p. 241. For examples: 1QM 16:11; 1QS 3:20-3; 1QpHab. 7:8. Cerfaux emphasizes 1QpHab. 7:5, "The Master of Justice to whom God *gave to know all the mysteries* (*rzy*) of his servants the prophets." However, the Qumran author is echoing Amos 3:7 where the original was *sôd*, a singular (note 80, above). As for Cerfaux' first point, the presence of distinctly Pauline influences on Mark's Gospel has been denied in investigations such as that by Martin Werner, *Der Einfluss paulinischer Theologie im Markusevangelium* (Giessen, 1923).

[104] As we have seen, *sôd* at Qumran is a synonym for *rāz*, often used in parallelism with it (1QH 4:27-8 and 11:9-10), or interchanged for it in set expressions. Much more than *rāz*, *sôd* is the key word in the genesis of the Semitic notion of divine mysteries.

its power on earth among different types of men. The mystery that Jesus reveals to his disciples[105] involves God's plan of salvation for men in the kingdom.[106] It has been suggested that the Synoptic use of *mystērion* is like that of Daniel and the apocalypses. L. Bouyer writes: ". . . the reference is to the interpretation of enigmatic symbols, in this case the parables of the Kingdom."[107] However, if we analyze the Synoptic statement carefully, we can see that the *mystērion* has no intrinsic connection with the parabolic form of teaching.[108] We might schematize the opposition of the various elements in Mark 4:11 thus:

A. The mystery of the kingdom of God	A. Everything
B. is granted	B. is
C. to you (disciples)	C. to those who are outside
D. (by Jesus' direct explanation).	D. in parables.

Thus, we should avoid exaggerating the similarity between the use of *mystērion* here and the method of revealing divine secrets through enigmatic symbols which is found in the apocalypses.

The real parallel to the Synoptic usage is where divine providence and its workings in reference to man's salvation are referred to as mysteries. We shall treat the mystery of God's redemptive plan of salvation in Jesus Christ more fully when we deal with Paul. But we may recall here Enoch 41:1 where Enoch sees "all the mysteries of the heavens and how the kingdom is divided; and the deeds of men, how they are weighed on the scale"[109]—a reference to God's kingdom as a mystery, in a context dealing with judgment on man's deeds. The idea that, to some extent, evil can impede good in the world (as the briars and the stony soil prevent the seed of the parable from bearing fruit) until God's judgment is part of "the

105 To be exact, Mark speaks of giving the disciples the mystery; and Matthew and Luke speak of giving the knowledge of the mystery.
106 Taylor (cited above, n. 102), p. 255; Lagrange, *Matthieu*, p. 258. Bornkamm, *TDNT* (cited above, n. 1), p. 819, says that the mystery is that Jesus is the Messiah, and that in Jesus the kingdom of God has entered time.
107 *"Mystērion"* in *Mystery and Mysticism* (New York: Philosophical Library, 1956), p. 22. Also H. von Soden, "Mysterion und Sacramentum in den ersten zwei Jahrhunderten der Kirche," *ZNW*, 12 (1911), p. 198, feels that the *rāz* of Daniel 2 is the general source of the NT *mystērion*, and especially of the mystery of the kingdom. This neglects too much of the other Semitic evidence. Von Soden's whole treatment is marred by over-insistence on the eschatological nature of the Christian mystery—see Deden (cited above, n. 1), p. 422.
108 We follow here the excellent study by J. A. Baird, "A Pragmatic Approach to Parable Exegesis," *JBL*, 76 (1957), p. 202.
109 Cf. note 60 above.

mystery of the times [*r'z' dzbn'*]" of II Baruch 81:4. The fact that the righteous are deceived by the evil angel is for Qumran "according to the mysteries of God [*rzy'l*] until the final time set by him" (1QS 3:20-23). Thus it is no novelty to Hebrew thought that the varied success of God's kingdom on earth is seen as a divine mystery.

Much has been made of the fact that the mystery of the kingdom has been clearly revealed to the disciples but not to outsiders, except under the veil of parables.[110] If we survey the Semitic concept of mystery, this attitude is almost what we would expect. In Numbers 12:8 God said of Moses: "Face to face do I speak with him and not in riddles [LXX: *ainigmata*]." In the apocalyptic books, the mysterious visions are offered to only very few; e.g., II Baruch 48:2-3, "You do not reveal your mysteries to many." Ezra's mysteries are to be taught only to the wise whose hearts can comprehend them (IV Ezra 12:36-37). The Qumran community's special mystery, the correct interpretation of the Law, is not to be given to outsiders.[111]

The reason for the divine *disciplina arcani* [discipline and restriction in passing on the secret] is clear in part: such intimate revelations of God's plan would be wasted on sinners whose eyes have been blinded by ignorance and prejudice. Both Enoch 80:7 and 1QS 5:11 show that sinners are not really interested in learning the divine mysteries. In part, however, the selection of those to whom the revelation of the mysteries is given touches on the question of God's predilection, a mystery that has not been revealed to men. Nevertheless, we should not overemphasize Jesus' denying to outsiders a knowledge of the mystery of the kingdom. After all, the Synoptic passage emphasizes the positive side—revelation to the disciples.[112] And even to outsiders the mystery is at least *given*; and

110 Both Dodd, p. 4, and Jeremias (both cited above, n. 101), p. 18, find it difficult to accept this as the authentic pedagogy of Jesus. Yet Baird (cited above, n. 108), pp. 205-07, has made a statistical count of the Synoptic parables attributed to Jesus: two thirds of the parables are explained by Jesus; but few of these explanations are given to those outside the group of disciples. And those parables which are explained to outsiders *do not deal with the kingdom*. Thus, seemingly, Jesus did not explain the parables dealing with the kingdom to outsiders, unless we are to presume an exceedingly technical rearrangement of the whole parable tradition by the Synoptics.

111 Cf. note 83 above.

112 Cerfaux (cited above, n. 101), p. 243: "The existence of a class of underprivileged is only the shadow born of the light, and in fact, proving its existence—the necessary consequence of election."

the parables which cloak it are not meaningless narration.[113] The parable gives some knowledge of the kingdom of God without completely unveiling it. The complete unveiling will come not so much by way of added revelation, as of added perception gained through faith, so that the hearers may comprehend what they have already heard. If they take the advice of Sirach (39:2-7), they will seek out "the secrets of proverbs," and busy themselves with "the hidden meanings of parables," and thus receive of God knowledge to "meditate on his mysteries."

2. THE APOCALYPSE OF JOHN

In the Apocalypse we have the only other non-Pauline occurrences of *mystērion*. The first occurs in the opening revelation of Alpha and Omega (1:20) who appears holding seven stars in his right hand and surrounded by seven lampstands. He tells John:

(19) Write then the things that you have seen, both what exists now and what will take place hereafter. (20) The *mystērion* of the seven stars which you have seen in my right hand and the seven golden lampstands is this: the seven stars are the angels of the seven churches, and the seven lampstands are the seven churches.

It is difficult to find the exact English equivalent of *mystērion* here; perhaps "secret, symbolic meaning" is a good approximation. The term has the same twofold meaning that *rāz* (LXX: *mystērion*) has in chapter 2 of Daniel: both the form of the vision and its content are mysteries. A careful reading of Daniel will show that the form of the vision is a mystery because it is a communication from God in a supernatural manner, and contains a complicated series of symbols. In turn, the content of the vision, i.e., what is signified by the symbols, is itself a mystery because it refers to something which has a special role in God's mysterious providence.

The similar use of mystery in Daniel and the Apocalypse is just another instance of the recognized connection between the two books. Of course, the same use of mystery is found in Enoch and

---

[113] Bornkamm, *TDNT* (cited above, n. 1), p. 818. At the beginning of the parable the people were often told to what it refers: "The kingdom of heaven is like. . . ." Siegman (cited above, n. 101), p. 176, insists that the Synoptic passages may *not* be rendered: "Everything is in riddles." Rather it is a question of indirect revelation. This point is more forceful if the final verse of the Synoptic passage (Mark 4:12 and parallels) was once independent and does not really interpret Jesus' purpose in using parables.

in the Apocalypses of Baruch and IV Ezra, with the slight difference that in these other apocalypses the interpreter of the symbol is often an angel rather than God himself. Even the symbols which are the vehicles of mysterious meaning in Apocalypse 1:20 are already familiar to us in Semitic mystery passages (albeit with a different meaning; apocalypses reuse old symbols but adapt them to the situation at hand). The use of definite numbered series, like the seven (stars) here, is a favorite device in symbolic mystery visions; e.g., in III Baruch 1:8, Baruch is taken on a tour through the seven heavens to be shown the "mysteries of God"; in Enoch 52:2, Enoch sees the "mysteries of heaven" which consist of six metallic mountains; and of course Daniel's mystery includes a number of kingdoms. As for the stars, Enoch's vision of the mysteries of heaven (43:1-4) includes stars which have names given them by God: the names of the stars, we are told, are the names of the saints who dwell on earth. In the Apocalypse the stars are angels.[114] The lamps-churches symbol is but the earthly parallel to the stars-angels of the churches in heaven.

Another occurrence of *mystērion* in the same vein is Apocalypse 17:5, 7. In the description of the sumptuously bedecked prostitute astride the scarlet beast, we are told:

(5) And on her forehead a name was written, *mystērion,* Babylon the great, mother of the harlots and of the abominations of the earth. (6) . . and I was greatly amazed and puzzled when I saw her. (7) And the angel said to me: "Why are you puzzled? I will tell you the *mystērion* of the woman and of the beast that is carrying her."

Again *mystērion* can be translated as a "secret, symbolic meaning." Here, as in the pseudepigraphical apocalypses, the interpreter is an angel. And again the symbols are familiar. For a name as a "mystery," not only do we have the above-mentioned stars of Enoch, but also the "hidden name" mentioned in the heavenly oath of Enoch 69:14. In both the Enoch passages, the mysterious meaning of the name has a good connotation; in the Apocalypse, the name is evil. As for the mystery of the beast, the explanation of Leviathan and Behemoth in Enoch 60:10 is called a mystery; and in III Baruch 3, one of the "mysteries of God" is the dragon of evil.

---

[114] The angels of the churches are reminiscent of Daniel's guardian angels of the nations (10:13; 12:1), and Qumran's great emphasis on angelic protection of the sect. In Enoch 86:1 and 88:3, the bad angels are the stars fallen from heaven.

A final occurrence of *mystērion* is Apocalypse 10:7, where the angel standing on the sea and land swears:

(6) . . . There shall be no more interval of time, (7) but at the time when the seventh angel speaks, when he is about to sound the trumpet, then is God's *mystērion* completed, as he announced to his servants, the prophets.

Here we have a different use of mystery—no longer a symbol, but the mysterious will of God for the end of time. H. B. Swete remarks that the mystery of God here is perhaps even wider than the Synoptic usage, " . . . including the whole purpose of God in the evolution of human history."[115] It is the definitive establishment of God's kingdom.

The last phrase is clearly a reminiscence of Amos 3:7, that God will not act "unless he has revealed his secret counsel (*sôd*) to his servants, the prophets." As we have seen (p. 24 above), this same passage occurs at Qumran (1QpHab. 7:1-5) where we are told that God did not reveal the fulfillment of the end to Habakkuk, but that he did reveal to the Teacher of Righteousness all the mysteries (*rzy*) of the words of his servants, the prophets. However, as the Qumran expositor noted, God had delayed this final period beyond prophetic expectation. The Apocalypse now tells us that at the seventh trumpet the delay is over, and God's secret plan is completed. In Enoch too there are references to the last judgment as a mystery.[116] II Baruch has this use of mystery also, coupled with the announcement (85:10) that the "coming of the times is almost here"—a close parallel in idea to the first part of our Apocalypse passage. IV Ezra 14:5 tells us that God showed Moses "the mystery of the times and the end of times."[117] We shall have occasion to return to this aspect of mystery later.

3. THE SECOND EPISTLE TO THE THESSALONIANS

In this epistle *mystērion* occurs once—in 2:7—where Paul tells the community that they must not be worried about the return of

---

[115] *The Apocalypse* (3rd ed.; London: Macmillan, 1911), p. 130; see also L. Cerfaux and J. Cambier, *L'Apocalypse* (Paris: Cerf, 1955), p. 87.

[116] Cf. pp. 17–18 above.

[117] Cf. p. 21 and n. 73 above.

Jesus. The day of the Lord will not come until the apostasy takes place, and there is revealed the man of lawlessness, the son of perdition:[118]

(6) And you know what is restraining [*to katechon*] him now from making his appearance in his time. (7) For the *mystērion* of lawlessness is already at work; but only when he who restrains [*ho katechōn*] it at present is got out of the way, will there 'be revealed the lawless one whom the Lord Christ will destroy with the breath of his mouth, and annihilate when he appears at his second coming.

B. Rigaux claims the *mystērion* in this passage is tantamount to "secretly."[119] For him, the secret movement of lawlessness is opposed to the brilliant openness of Christ's coming. Certainly there may be an element of secrecy of action. However, we believe that *mystērion* is employed primarily to signify the mysterious disposition of divine providence whereby evil is allowed to exist and work in the world. The economy of evil (like the economy of divine salvation) is a mystery because it is the work of a supernatural being, beyond human knowledge.[120] We have here the mystery of a kingdom—Satan's, not God's [121]—and it is a kingdom that is continually operative in this world until Jesus Christ destroys it at his coming.

[118] Roland E. Murphy, in *Biblica*, 39 (1958), p. 66, n. 4, suggests that *ho huios tēs apōleias* reflects the Qumran *bn(y) šḥt* (CD 6:15; 13:14; and *'nšy šḥt* in 1QS 9:16 and 22:10,19). For *ho anthrōpos tēs anomias* (a variant has *hamartias*) we suggest, perhaps, the frequent *bn(y) 'wl*. In the past, a Hebrew equivalent of *'yš bly'l* has been suggested; but by Paul's time, as Qumran witnesses, *Bly'l* was too much of a proper name. Now *anomia* frequently represents *pš'*, as we shall see; but it need not always represent the same Hebrew term. A good backing for our suggestion of *bn(y) 'wl* is Ps. 89:23 where *ben 'awlâ* is rendered in the LXX as *huios anomias*. Comparable to Qumran's opposition of *bny 'wl* and *bny ṣdq*, we have in II Cor. 6:14-5 (see below, n. 121) *anomia* opposed to *dikaiosynē*. Thus we have good Qumran equivalents for both Pauline expressions for the evil man.

[119] *Les Épîtres aux Thessaloniciens* (Paris: Gabalda, 1956), p. 272.

[120] As both von Soden (cited above, n. 107), p. 194, and Deden (cited above, n. 1), p. 411, point out, the eschatological context also surrounds the Satanic activity with mystery atmosphere.

[121] In 2:9 Paul mentions "the working of Satan." This belief that there is a supreme evil spirit at work behind the lawlessness in the world is also found elsewhere. Eph. 2:2 speaks of "the leadership of the prince of the air, the spirit now at work in the children of wrath." II Cor. 6:14-15 (a passage with numerous Qumran parallels) sets up Belial as the chief opponent of Christ, and associates him with lawlessness:

What partnership can there be between *dikaiosynē* and *anomia*?
What communion between light and darkness?
What accord between Christ and Belial?

See J. A. Fitzmyer, "Qumrân and the Interpolated Paragraph in 2 Cor 6,14-7,1," *CBQ*, 23 (1961), pp. 271-80.

There is no perfect parallel in the NT for the ideas of II Thessalonians, although there are some similarities in the Apocalypse. Recently Qumran has supplied us with a remarkable conceptual parallel. (We do not claim any *direct* influence of Qumran thought on Paul; we use the Dead Sea Scrolls as a witness to ideas current in the pre-Christian Jewish world.) We may remember that for Qumran (1QS 3:20-3; 4:18) mankind lives under the aegis of two spirits, one evil and one good, locked in continual opposition. The evil spirit is permitted to function "according to the mysteries of God until the final time set by him." Thus there is a real economy of evil at work, restrained by the spirit of truth.[122]

Not only is the general framework of Pauline thought paralleled at Qumran, but even the very terminology seems to occur. We have seen that several times at Qumran the phrase *rzy pš'* occurs[123]; and about twenty times the LXX renders *pš'* by *anomia*—thus we may well have the Hebrew original of the Pauline *mystērion tēs anomias*. It is on the basis of this Qumran evidence that we reject the interpretation that *mystērion* is used in the Thessalonians *only* to signify the secrecy of evil as opposed to the openness of Christ's coming. In both cases mystery seems to have a more metaphysical bent: Satan's economy of damnation. This is well expressed in another Qumran passage (IQM 14:9): " . . . against the dominion of Belial and against his diabolic mysteries (*rzy šṭmtw*)."

4. THE FIRST EPISTLE TO THE CORINTHIANS

We next turn to the five (or six) occurrences of *mystērion* in I Corinthians. The most important is that of 2:7, where Paul tells his community that he did not come to them with lofty words, but with the power of the Spirit to preach Jesus Christ crucified:

(5) . . . that your faith might not rest in the wisdom of men but in the power of God. (6) Wisdom, however, we do impart among those that are mature [*teleioi*]. Yet we impart a wisdom not of this world nor of the doomed powers of this world, (7) but a hidden wisdom of God *en mysterio,* [a wisdom] which God predetermined before the ages for our glory, (8) which no one of the rulers of this

---

[122] 1QS 3:21: "In the hand of the angel of darkness is all the domination (*mmšlt*) over the sons of evil (*bny 'wl*) and in the way of darkness they walk." There is some similarity between Qumran's picture of the opposition to this evil domination, an opposition supplied by the angel of light, and the work of the restrainer in Paul.

[123] See pp. 28–29 above, also n. 95.

world had known. . . . (9) But, as it is written: "Things which the eye has never seen, and the ear never heard, and which have never come into human imagination—these things which God has prepared for those who love him," (10) God has indeed revealed to us through the Spirit. For the Spirit fathoms all things, even the depths of God.

The exact meaning of *en mystēriō* here is difficult. In some way it modifies the hidden (*apokekrymmenē*) wisdom which Paul is presenting to the mature. The R.S.V. translates it as an adjective: "the secret and hidden wisdom of God." Yet the introduction of *mystērion* in a separate prepositional phrase seems to indicate a special role for it in Paul's mind. Dupont and Lyonnet would translate the phrase as: "in announcing a mystery."[124] Nevertheless, there is truth in C. L. Mitton's idea that the chief interest in 2:7 is wisdom, and that the reference to mystery is secondary.[125]

What is this hidden wisdom that Paul speaks of *en mystēriō*? It is clearly wisdom that stems from divine insight as opposed to worldly wisdom. And it is more than mere knowledge, for it is a reality predestined from all time. As the succeeding verses make clear, it is the economy of salvation prepared beforehand for those whom God loves, and now at last revealed. In other words, *sophia en mystēriō* covers much of the same conceptual territory that we shall later see covered by *mystērion* alone.[126] Paul is groping here to subsume the plan and its realization under one phrase.[127] It may be suggested that if here he did not use *mystērion* alone, as he would later, it was because the combination of wisdom and mystery was so traditional. In Sirach 4:18, Wisdom is an agent of God in revealing secrets; in 14:20, happy is the man who meditates on Wisdom and her secrets; in Wisd. Sol. 6:22, the very origin of Wisdom is called a mystery; and in Wisd. Sol. 7:21, Wisdom

---

[124] J. Dupont, *Gnosis* (Paris: Gabalda, 1949), p. 137, n. 1; S. Lyonnet, *Biblica*, 35 (1954), p. 495, n. 1.
[125] *The Epistle to the Ephesians* (Oxford: Clarendon, 1951), p. 87.
[126] *Ibid.* Deden (cited above, n. 1), pp. 412-13, has studied *sophia* in its twenty-six Pauline occurrences. He distinguishes three phases: the wisdom eternally hidden in God; revelation of this wisdom in Christ; participation of Christians in this wisdom. "The connection between *sophia Theou* and *mystērion* is verified in all three types of the *sophia*." As we shall point out below (p. 49), if we read *mystērion* in I Cor. 2:1, then "the mystery of God" is almost interchangeable with "the wisdom of God" in 1:24.
[127] Prümm, "Phänomenologie" (cited above, n. 98), pp. 146-48, makes the point that mystery is used here, not only because of the hidden nature of the plan, but also because the revelation and realization of the plan required a marvelous and mysterious use of divine power. Realization is an integral part of the Pauline *mystērion*.

teaches things that are secret. Of course, wisdom is personified in these passages, whereas in Paul it is not; but that may be the very reason why he soon shifted the accent from wisdom to mystery.

A great deal of attention has been paid to the fact that Paul imparts his wisdom to the *teleioi*. We shall not take time to discuss the idea that these *teleioi* are comparable to the initiates of the mystery religions.[128] As the contrast with babes and children in 14:20 shows, *teleios* here means mature or adult. What Paul means, then, is that only the spiritually mature will understand the wisdom that he preaches. It is not a question of a new or additional doctrine reserved for the few, but of a mystery which requires personal reflection accompanied by spiritual growth. This is why Paul stresses —in 2:10— that all these things which constitute the wisdom *en mystēriō* have been revealed *through the Spirit*,[129] for the maturity required to understand the mystery is in part the work of the Spirit. We might add that this meaning of *teleios* fits very well the LXX use of it as a translation for Hebrew *šālēm* in the expression "keeping one's heart perfectly true to the Lord."[130]

The idea of revealing the profound knowledge of a mystery only to those who are spiritually ready for it is well attested in the Semitic world. For instance, in 1QS 4:22 we see that insight into the knowledge of God and into the wisdom of the sons of heaven is given to the upright and the perfect (*tāmîm*) of way, just as Paul's wisdom of God is given to the mature. The secrets of the Qumran sect are not to be revealed to mere beginners (CD 15:10), but only to those who choose the way, each according to his spirit, to make them wise in God's marvelous and true mysteries (1QS 9:18). And we remember the words of IV Ezra 12:36-37, concerning the divine mysteries: "And you shall teach them to

[128] See Kennedy (cited above, n. 99), pp. 130 ff.; Dupont, *Gnosis* (cited above, n. 124), p. 151, n. 1; and K. Maly, *Mündige Gemeinde: Untersuchungen zur pastoralen Führung des Apostels Paulus im 1. Korintherbrief* ("Stuttgarter Biblische Monographien," 2; Stuttgart: Verlag Katholisches Bibelwerk, 1967), pp. 33 ff., especially n. 33. C. K. Barrett, *A Commentary on the First Epistle to the Corinthians* ("Harper's NT Commentaries"; New York: Harper and Row, 1968) thinks it doubtful whether the term "mystery" in Paul ever alludes to "the 'mystery' rites into which the *mature, teleioi*, had been initiated" (pp. 70-1) and holds that *teleioi* here means "mature Christians" (p. 68).

[129] See C. Spicq, *Les Épîtres Pastorales* (2nd ed.; Paris: Gabalda, 1947), *Excursus* V, p. 123. Also J. Schneider, " '*Mystērion*' im Neuen Testament" (cited above, n. 27), p. 267. The importance of the Spirit leads to Paul's equation of the *teleioi* with the *pneumatikoi* (2:13 ff.).

[130] Frequent in I Kings (8:61; 11:4; 15:3, 14). Other Hebrew words translated by *teleios* are *tām* and *tāmîm* (e.g., Sirach 44:17).

the wise among your people whose hearts you know can comprehend and keep these mysteries."[131] In Sirach, Wisdom reveals her secrets only to those of whose goodness she is convinced.[132] More citations may be found in our treatment of the Synoptic passage where the mysteries of the kingdom of God are reserved to the disciples (see above, pp. 35–36).

There are Semitic parallels too for other features of our I Corinthians passage. Paul's wisdom is not of this world nor is it understood by those of the world. In reference to Daniel's interpretation of Nebuchadnezzar's dream, we hear: "Wise men . . . cannot show to the king the mystery which the king has asked, but there is a God in heaven who reveals mysteries" (Dan. 2:27-28). Again at Qumran we have a very interesting parallel: "Sound wisdom which is hidden from wise men, . . . a fountain of glory [hidden] from the worldly assembly: God has granted these to those whom he selected as an eternal possession" (1QS 11:6-7). As for the mystery's being hidden from all ages, the same idea is found in Enoch 48:6; 62:7 and Wisd. Sol. 6:22 (p. 10 above).

Finally we wish to point out parallels to the role of the "Spirit" in revealing the wisdom *en mystēriō* (although not, of course, in the Christian sense meant by Paul).[133] It is interesting to compare the role of the Spirit with that of Wisdom in Wisd. Sol. 8:4, where Wisdom initiates men into the knowledge of God and reveals to them the mysteries of God (also Sirach 4:18; 14:20-21). In other Jewish mystery passages we find mention of "the spirit." In Sirach 48:24-25, we are told that Isaiah looked into the future with the aid of a powerful spirit (*rûah—pneuma*) and foretold hidden things not yet fulfilled. Nebuchadnezzar says to Daniel (Dan.

[131] Deden (cited above, n. 1), p. 432, distinguishes very sharply between Paul's outlook and that of the Jewish apocalypses on those who are privileged to receive the mystery. It is true that with Paul it is a question of growth of perception in doctrine already revealed, and with others it is a real limitation of revelation. However, for both, it is only the elect of God who are the original recipients of the mysteries (people like Enoch, Ezra, Baruch; and in Paul's case, the apostles). And secondly, the limit on those to whom the mystery is to be transmitted is, in both cases, of a moral nature: only the spiritually wise receive the mystery.

[132] Sirach 4:18. Also to be noted is Sirach 3:21-23 where, for those who are incapable, there is a positive discouragement from investigating the hidden things of God. See pp. 8–9 above.

[133] That the spirit in I Cor. 2:10 is the Holy Spirit is generally conceded (E.-B. Allo, *Première Épître aux Corinthiens* [2nd ed.; Paris: Gabalda, 1956], p. 45.) As Prümm, "Mystères" (cited above, n. 45), col. 197 remarks, the precise meaning of "spirit" does not affect the problem of *mystērion*.

4:6[9]): "I know that the spirit [*rûaḥ—pneuma*] of the holy God [gods?] is in you, and no mystery is difficult for you." And 1QH 12:11-12 says: "And I, endowed with wisdom, have known you, O my God, through the spirit which you have given me; and I have heard what is certain in your marvelous mysteries through your holy spirit." In these examples it is difficult to assay the exact connotation of "spirit," but they represent possible raw material for Pauline theological phraseology.

A second mention of mystery occurs in I Cor. 4:1. Flailing the Corinthians for their factionalism, Paul says:

(1) Thus let men regard us: as servants of Christ and stewards of [the] *mysteries of God.*

Unfortunately, there is nothing in the context to specify the meaning of "mysteries." It should be noted, however, that the word is used in the plural—one of the three examples of the plural in Paul, all in I Corinthians. On the one hand, the plural may indicate a more general scope than the great mystery (singular) of salvation mentioned elsewhere by Paul.[134] Or, on the other hand, the plural may simply show that Paul, at the beginning of his literary career, had not yet fixed his usage. Prümm maintains that the mysteries of 4:1 stand in connection with the theme of salvation in Christ, and are just a literary variant of the great mystery.[135]

What is of particular interest here is that God has appointed the apostles as *oikonomoi* of the mysteries of God. As Paul employs the term here, he seems to mean servants of Christ dispensing to other servants the mysteries of the Gospel.[136] The entrusting

[134] So Deden (cited above, n. 1), p. 410; and Allo (cited above, n. 133), p. 68.
[135] "Phänomenologie" (cited above, n. 98), p. 139.
[136] For the meaning of *oikonomos* in the NT, see E. Hatch, *Essays in Biblical Greek* (Oxford: Clarendon, 1889), pp. 62-63. Kennedy, (cited above, n. 99), p. 125, refutes the idea that these caretakers of the mysteries are similar to the initiating priests of the mystery religions. Their role is closer to that of the OT prophets who have been entrusted with the mysteries of the divine assembly (*sôd*). J. Reumann, " 'Stewards of God'— Pre-Christian Religious Application of *Oikonomos* in Greek," *JBL*, 77 (1958), pp. 339-49, states that "it is the background in Greco-Roman life and the use of the term with already existing religious connotations which provide the immediate and most obvious insight into Paul's designation of himself and others as 'stewards of God' and his mysteries" (p. 349). In a later article, "*Oikonomia*-terms in Paul in Comparison with Lucan *Heilsgeschichte*," *NTS*, 13 (1966-67), pp. 147-67, Reumann shows that Hellenistic Judaism made common use of *oikonomia* terminology and that

of mysteries to one man for the sake of others is nothing new. The Qumran psalmist (1QH 2:13-14) thanks God that He has set him up as a banner for the elect, and the interpreter of knowledge in His marvelous mysteries, to test the men of truth. In other words, he is to interpret the mysteries of God for the sectarians who must accept his interpretation. The Pauline expression "mysteries of God" echoes the *rzy 'l* familiar at Qumran; and paralleling the *oikonomoi*, we have in 1Q36:16, "men in custody of your mysteries [*'nšy mšmrt lrzykh*]."

Before we leave chapter 4, we should take notice of a verse which appears a few lines later. Paul does not really care what the world thinks of him as a steward. The important thing is the judgment of the Lord, who, at his coming, "will bring to light the things hidden [*krypta*] in darkness and will disclose the counsels [*boulai*] of the heart."[137] This is a thought found also in Rom. 2:16: there will be a day when, according to Paul's gospel, God will judge the secrets (*krypta*) of man through Jesus Christ. This is a direct echo of Jewish ideas. Sirach stressed God's ability to see secret wickedness,[138] and promised that He would eventually reveal the secrets (*krypta*—1:30) of sinners. In Enoch we are told that when the Righteous One shall appear, "The secrets of the just shall be revealed, and the sinners shall be judged"; and "His mouth shall pour forth all the secrets of wisdom and counsel" (38:3; 51:3).

A third use of *mystērion* is in I Cor. 13:2 in the hymn of love. Paul presents a list of things which, even if he possessed them, would be in vain without love:

(2) Suppose even that I have the gift of prophecy, and that I am acquainted with *all the mysteries* and all knowledge, and that I have complete faith such as to move mountains, but I do not have love—I am nothing.

oikonomos became a loan word in late (Mishnaic) Hebrew (pp. 151-52). As for the present passage, he denies mystery-cult influence and thinks that Paul's usage must be related to his understanding of his apostolic work (pp. 160-61). Cf. also "Heilsgeschichte in Luke: Some Remarks on Its Background and Comparison with Paul," in *Studia Evangelica IV* (ed. F. L. Cross; "Texte und Untersuchungen," 102; Berlin: Akademie-Verlag, 1968), pp. 86-115.

[137] 4:5. We call attention to the parallelism of *boulai* and *krypta*, remembering that *sôd*, "secret counsel," is translated by *boulē* in the LXX, e.g., Prov. 11:13: *mᵉgalleh sôd—apokalyptei boulas*.

[138] 16:17 ff.; 17:15 ff.; 23:18 ff.; 39:19.

There is no indication of the exact content of the mysteries here; rather "all the mysteries" seems to be an expression for the sum of religious knowledge attainable on earth.[139] Verses 9 ff. explain why this knowledge is not as important as love: it is imperfect, partial.[140]

In the Semitic background we call attention to the expression "*all* mysteries." When Enoch receives a revelation of divine mysteries, it is frequently said: "And he showed me all the mysteries of . . ."[141] This is tantamount to an expression of the depth of knowledge revealed to him by God; it does not mean that there are no other mysteries that he has not seen. As he confesses to God (63:3), "All your mysteries are deep and numberless." Sirach 43:32 has the same idea: there are mysteries greater than the ones that have been seen, for after all we have seen but a few of God's works. Thus a man may say that God had shown him all the mysteries; and yet, still recognize that his knowledge is imperfect[142]—something not very far from Paul's idea. Naturally, we do not expect a parallel to Paul's evaluation of love over knowledge, since that emphasis seems to be preeminently Christian.

A fourth occurrence is that of I Cor. 14:2, which praises prophecy over the gift of "speaking in a tongue":

(2) For the one who speaks in a tongue does not talk to men, but to God; for not a soul understands him, but through the Spirit he utters *mysteries.*

---

[139] Kennedy (cited above, n. 99), p. 168, points out that, in the context of charisma, there can be little doubt that the knowledge of all the mysteries is religious knowledge. Bouyer (cited above, n. 107), p. 22, would identify the mysteries here as "the general sense of a secret concerning the end of the world." This is possible (see the Qumran usage of "all the mysteries" in n. 142 below); but there is no real evidence for it.

[140] See 13:12, "We see now in a mirror, under the form of an enigma, then face to face." For this translation, see Dupont, *Gnosis* (cited above, n. 124), p. 137, n. 1. This text is a reminiscence of Num. 12:8, "And God spoke to Moses face to face, and not *di' ainigmatōn.*"

[141] Enoch 41:1; 52:2; 61:5; 63:3; 68:5; 71:4. We are told in 16:3 (p. 14 above) that all the mysteries had not been revealed to the fallen angels. In IV Ezra 10:38, we find what is, perhaps, a more accurate idiom: the Most High has revealed *many* mysteries to him.

[142] There are some possible exceptions where the *all* may have to be taken literally. In Enoch 49:2 and 51:3, the Elect One, the Son of Man, is mighty in "all the secrets of righteousness," and on the day of judgment shall pour forth "all the secrets of wisdom and counsel." Because of the preeminent role of this figure in Enoch, we may have a statement of absolute knowledge. At Qumran, God revealed to the Teacher of Righteousness "all the mysteries (*kwl rzy*) of the words of his servants, the prophets" (1QpHab. 7:4-5). How literally this is to be taken depends on how one interprets the role of the Teacher.

In this very difficult passage, we shall confine ourselves to the problem of the exact force of the last clause. It may be an explanation of the preceding clause, meaning: ". . . for he speaks mysteriously by the Spirit."[143] Or it may stress the import of the message: no one understands him even though by divine aid he speaks mysteries. The first interpretation ("mysteriously") makes good sense, and is certainly possible. However, the expression "by the Spirit" inclines us to the second interpretation whereby "mysteries" mean hidden truths. We refer the reader to our discussion of I Corinthians 2 above (pp. 42–44) where we cited passages from Sirach, Enoch, and Qumran all dealing with the knowledge of mysteries "through the spirit." In any case our text is not very important for the Pauline *mystērion*.

A fifth occurrence of *mystērion* is 15:51. Speaking of the resurrection of the dead, Paul tells the Corinthians that perishable flesh and blood will not inherit the kingdom of heaven:

(51) Look here, I tell you *a mystery*: we shall not all die, but we shall all be changed—(52) in a moment, in the twinkling of an eye, at the last trumpet. For it will sound, and the dead will be raised up to life eternal; and as for us, we shall be changed.

The mystery here seems to be that all the elect of God, dead or alive, will in the end be transformed so that they may inherit the kingdom of God.[144] This mystery, brought forward by Paul, solves the problem of how flesh and blood can enter heaven.

We have in the Semitic background several occurrences of "mystery" in reference to the day of judgment and the resurrection of the dead. The "mysteries of God"—of which the wicked are ignorant in Wisd. Sol. 2:22—are the rewards of the just in the after-life.[145]

---

143 Allo (cited above, n. 133), p. 356, "If Paul calls these exclamations 'mysteries,' it is rather because of the inaccessible form of the language than because of the content." Robertson and Plummer, *I Corinthians* (ICC, 1911), p. 306, take just the opposite view. Barrett (cited above, n. 128) says the meaning is "secrets" or hidden truths.

144 Allo (cited above, n. 133), p. 432 Is this usage of *mystērion* to be grouped with those where *mystērion* refers to the great plan of salvation; or is it a question of particular charismatic knowledge? Hatch (cited above, n. 136), pp. 58-59, favors the former; Deden (cited above, n. 1), p. 410, the latter. Schneider (cited above, n. 27), pp. 267-68, calls attention to the fact that the possibility or hope of attaining to glory is frequently connected with the great Pauline mystery, and that the mystery of 15:51 is the final stage of the divine plan, i.e., glory.

145 Cf. n. 39 above.

47

We may recall, too, the vision of Enoch 61 (pp. 17–18 above) where angels gather the measurements of the just: these measurements shall reveal the mysteries of the resting places of the dead, so that they may return and take their stand on the day of the Elect One. One passage in Enoch (103:2 ff.) is worth special attention. Faced with the problem of the death of the righteous, Enoch says: "I know a mystery: . . . all goodness and joy and glory are prepared for those who have died in righteousness. . . . Your lot is far beyond the lot of the living." While there is no exact parallel to the point that Paul is making (i.e., that even the living will be changed), we find a good parallel for bringing forward private knowledge of a mystery as an explanation of problems concerning the judgment of the living and the dead.

We have left to the end of our treatment of the mystery passages in I Corinthians a possible occurrence of *mystērion* in 2:1, which is very closely related to 2:7, treated above.

(1) And when I came to you, brethren, I came without outstanding eloquence or knowledge, preaching to you *the mystery* [witness] *of God*.

The ms. evidence is divided on whether to read *mystērion* or *martyrion*, "witness," and no solution seems possible on textual grounds.[146] From the point of usage, *martyrion* is not used with "God" elsewhere; and the NT usually says, "for a witness of or against." *Mystērion* occurs with "God" twice (I Cor. 4:1; Rev. 10:17), and is frequently the object of a verb like "make known, speak."[147] The frequency of the expression "mysteries of God" at

---

146 Hitherto most critical editions of the Greek NT (e.g., Nestle, Merk) have favored *martyrion*, but the 1966 Bible Society edition (Aland) favors *mystērion* (so now R.S.V. and N.E.B. notes). While Barrett (cited above, n. 128) settles on *martyrion*, *mystērion* is preferred by such commentators as J. Weiss ("Meyer Kommentar," 1910), H. Lietzmann ("Handbuch zum NT," 1931), and J. Héring ("Commentaire du NT," 1948; Eng. trans., London: Epworth, 1962); so also G. Bornkamm, *TDNT, "mystērion"* (cited above, n. 1), p. 819, n. 141; U. Wilckens, *Weisheit und Torheit* (Tübingen: J. C. B. Mohr [Paul Siebeck], 1959), p. 45, n. 1; and R. Funk, *Language, Hermeneutic, and Word of God* (New York: Harper, 1966), p. 295, n. 82.

147 We take this opportunity to list some of the verbs and nouns that govern *mystērion* in the NT:

katangellein: here?; Col. 1:28   *lalein*: I Cor. 2:7; 14:2; Col. 4:3
legein—erō: I Cor. 15:51; Rev. 17:7   *idein*: Rev. 1:20
phaneroun: Rom. 16:25; Col. 1:26; 4:4   *synesis*: Eph. 3:4
gignōskein-epignōsis: Synoptics; Col. 2:2

Qumran also seems to favor the reading of *mystērion* here. In any case, *mystērion* in 2:1 would have the same meaning as the wisdom *en mystēriō* of 2:7. However, such a reading would make certain that *en mystēriō* is not merely a synonym for "secretly"; and we would have, already in this early epistle, a clear application of *mystērion* to the divine economy of salvation. The *mystērion* that Paul proclaims in 2:1 would be the same as what he preaches in 1:23-24, namely: "Christ crucified . . . the wisdom of God."

Mystērion does not occur in II Corinthians. But in 12:4, where Paul is narrating in the third person how he had a heavenly vision, there occurs an important text which we shall briefly consider:[148]

(4) that he was caught up to Paradise and heard secret words [*arrēta rēmata*] which man is not permitted to speak.

Since *arrētos* is used in the mystery religions for those things which are too sacred to tell the uninitiated, it is natural that this text has been used to prove Paul's dependence on mystery religions.[149] Actually, it is not clear whether Paul is actually forbidden to speak the secret words or is just incapable of describing in human terms the marvelous things he has seen. As for having

phōtizein: Eph. 3:9; I Cor. 4:5 (*krypta*)
apokalyptein-apokalypsis: Eph. 3:3-5; Rom. 16:25
gnōrizein: Rom. 16:26; Col. 1:27; Eph. 1:9; 3:3, 5, 10; 6:19
These words compare favorably with the words used in the Greek OT:
(*ap, par, pros*) *angellein*: II Macc. 13:21; Dan. 2:18; Wisd. Sol. 6:22
(*ana, apo*) *kalyptein*: Sirach 3:18 (suppletor); 22:22; 27:16, 17, 21; Dan. 2:28-29; Dan. (Theodotion) 2:19, 30, and 47
dēloun: Dan. 2:47   *ekphainein*: Dan. 2:19, 30, 47   *gignōskein*: Wisd. Sol. 2:22
A. D. Nock, "The Vocabulary of the New Testament," *JBL,* 52 (1933), pp. 131-39, shows how little vocabulary similarity there is with the mystery religions.

148 Two verses before, instead of "Paradise," Paul speaks of a "third heaven." This notion is found in Testament of Levi 2:8, in connection with declaring the mysteries of God to men; also the Apocalypse of Moses [called "The Books of Adam and Eve" in *AP* II, p. 151] 40:2. We might mention a curious use of *rēma krypton* in the LXX of Deut. 15:9, "Take care lest a secret word [Hebrew: base thought] enter your mind."

149 E.-B. Allo, *Seconde Épître aux Corinthiens* [2nd ed.; Paris: Gabalda, 1956], p. 306, speaks of Paul's "borrowing for once a term from the language of the mystery religions." C. Kerényi, *The Mysteries of the Kabeiroi,* reprinted in *The Mysteries* (Papers from the *Eranos Yearbooks,* 2), p. 37, stresses that the "secret" of the mystery religions had primarily the character of *arrēton*, the unutterable, and only subsequently the character of *aporrēton*, what is forbidden to tell.

heavenly visions, Paul's experience is certainly similar to the heavenly visions of mysteries entrusted to Enoch, Baruch, and Ezra (with accompanying injunctions of secrecy). In Enoch 69:14, a name is secret; thus there is an adequate parallel if the Pauline "secret words" is to be taken literally. All in all, it is well to be cautious about claiming that we must leave the Jewish world and enter the sphere of pagan Hellenistic culture in our search for the background of II Cor. 12:4.

5. THE EPISTLE TO THE ROMANS

The first of the two occurrences of *mystērion* in Romans is 11:25. Speaking of the conversion of the Gentiles, Paul suggests that one day the Jews will be converted too. He warns the Romans:

(25) For brethren, lest you think too much of yourselves, I do not want you ignorant of *this mystery*: only partial blindness has come upon Israel until all the nations shall have come in, (26) and then all Israel shall be saved.

Here again Paul clarifies a difficult theological problem by announcing a mystery he knows; but this mystery is closely connected with what we shall see to be Paul's favorite use of *mystērion*: the divine economy of redemption. It should be noted that this is the only place where the salvation of the Jews is emphasized as part of the mystery[150]; elsewhere the salvation of the Gentiles is given primary attention.

God's apparent rejection of Israel is also a mystery in IV Ezra. One of the mysteries revealed to Ezra (10:38 ff.) is that the vision he has seen of the suffering woman represents Zion, who, though now rejected, will again shine forth in glory after her exile. Of course, this mystery is under the form of a vision; but the content of the vision, God's mysterious plan for the spiritual renovation of Israel, is an apt precedent for Paul's usage. At Qumran, apparent rejection is a mystery on a more personal level. In 1QH 9:23-24

[150] Kennedy (cited above, n. 99), pp. 124-25, suggests that the obscure and paradoxical way in which the Jews will eventually be converted helps to make *mystērion* a fitting term here. Prümm, "Mystères" (cited above, n. 45), col. 223, holds that the enigma of Israel's rejection was resolved for Paul through a special revelation and a progressive comprehension of the mysterious predictions of the OT hidden under the veil of the typical or figurative sense (e.g., II Cor. 3:11 ff.). For *mystērion* used for a figurative sense of the OT, see Eph. 5:32 below. J. Munck, *Christ & Israel: an Interpretation of Romans 9-11* (Philadelphia: Fortress, 1967), pp. 131-32, refers it to "God's plan of salvation" at Rom. 11:25.

the psalmist sees his own chastisement as a mystery of divine wisdom, feeling sure that one day the chastisement will be a source of joy.[151] Thus, granted the originality of Paul's Christian outlook on salvation, there are good Jewish examples where apparent rejection is seen as a part of the divine mysteries.

A second passage in Romans is the parting salutation (16:25).[152] Paul gives his own closing blessing:

(25) To the one who has the power to strengthen you, in conformity with my gospel and the preaching of Jesus Christ, in conformity with a revelation of a *mystery* kept secret for long ages, (26) but now brought into the open; and by means of prophetic writings, according to the command of the eternal God, made known to all the Gentiles to [lead them to] the obedience of faith . . . be glory. . . .

In I Corinthians 2:7 we had the divine wisdom *en mystēriō,* which God had predetermined before all ages, revealed to us through the Spirit. Here it is the *mystērion* itself which was secret and is now brought to light. Moreover, the revelation of the mystery is in parallelism with the preaching of Christ (objective genitive).[153] In other words, for Paul, Christ's life and role in the salvation of men are the revelation of God's mysterious plan hidden from ages past. Thus this doxology supplies the first clear example of the equation of the *mystērion* and Christ, an equation which we shall see developed in the Captivity Epistles.[154]

[151] Perhaps we might also cite 1QM 16:11, where the soldiers of the armies of light are seen to fall by the mysteries (i.e., mysterious purpose) of God. One day the trials will result in victory.

[152] The question of whether chapter 16 as a whole and the doxology in 16:25-27 in particular were originally part of the Letter to the Romans is well known, and the arguments for answering in the negative are plausible. Of course, a negative answer still does not solve the further question of whether the respective material is Pauline. Kennedy (cited above, n. 99), p. 128, n. 1, refuses to discuss the doxology, since he does not believe such "mosaic work" can be the work of Paul. But Robinson, *Ephesians* (cited above, n. 27), p. 238, assures us that the use here of *mystērion* is "characteristically Pauline." At the other extreme, Mitton, *Ephesians* (cited above, n. 125), p. 257, uses Rom. 16:25 to help show that Eph. 3:20-21 is not an original composition of Paul but a mosaic from other works! In any case, we have a Christian use of *mystērion* consonant with Paul's theology.

[153] The passage in Romans loses some of its originality if we accept as authentic the reading *mystērion* in I Cor. 2:1, for as we pointed out (p. 49 above) that reading sets up an equivalence between proclaiming the mystery and preaching Christ crucified.

[154] William Sanday, *Romans* (ICC, 1901), p. 434, remarks that in I Corinthians the Apostle seems to be arriving at his understanding of the mystery; in the Captivity Epistles it is already full-blown; Romans provides an excellent transition. Obviously this progression depends on answering affirmatively the questions raised in note 152.

In treating I Corinthians we indicated Jewish parallels to some of the features that also appear in Romans; others are better treated later; but let us attend here to the role of the prophetic writings[155] in spreading the knowledge of the mystery. In the previous chapter of Romans, Paul has spoken at length of the salvation of the Gentiles, citing four passages from the OT which state that the Gentiles will worship God. Perhaps the conclusion of chapter 16 may be interpreted in the light of Paul's own use of OT prophecies: they help to make known the mystery because they show that the salvation of the Gentiles had always been intended by God. Christ had come and acted according to the prediction of the Scriptures.

The connection of the prophets with mysteries dates back to the role of the prophet as witness in the heavenly *sôd,* where he heard the secret counsels of God and conveyed them to men. That the prophets were vehicles of divine mysteries was not forgotten in later generations: Sirach 48:24-25 tells us that Isaiah foretold "hidden things not yet fulfilled"; and IV Ezra 14:5 says that God showed Moses the secrets of the times and the end of times. In fact, the pseudepigraphical apocalypses had a quasi-prophetic function; they were written down so that later generations might find therein the mysteries of God and understand them (Enoch 104: 10-12; IV Ezra 12:36-37). Qumran had its *pešarîm* which attempted to find in the mysterious words of the prophets lessons applicable to contemporary times. 1QpHab. 7:1-5 tells us that God did not reveal the exact fulfillment to Habakkuk; it was only to the Teacher of Righteousness that God revealed all the mysteries in the prophets' words. This is not far from Paul's claim that God has hidden his mysterious plan of salvation within the words of prophetic writings; but now, in the time of fulfillment, this mysterious plan is at last made clear (cf. also I Peter 1:10-12).

6. THE EPISTLE TO THE COLOSSIANS

The first two occurrences of *mystērion* are in 1:26-27. After glorifying Christ, the first-born of creation, Paul reminds the Colossians that he is suffering for their sake, and for the sake of Christ's body:

---

[155] That these refer to the OT prophecies and not contemporary Christian prophecies, cf. Lagrange, *Romans* (Paris: Gabalda, 1916), p. 379.

(24) . . . which is the Church, (25) of which I became a servant by virtue of the role in God's plan [*oikonomia tou Theou*] assigned to me for you: to make the message [*logos*] of God complete—(26) the *mystery* which has been hidden from the ages and generations of the past, but is now disclosed to his saints. (27) To them God wishes to show how rich in glory among the Gentiles is this *mystery*, i.e., Christ among you, the hope of glory. (28) It is he whom we proclaim, admonishing every man in all wisdom, so that we may bring forward every man as mature [*teleios*] in Christ.

We encounter elements here already familiar to us in the Pauline concept of mystery.[156] The *logos* or message of God is in apposition to the mystery, just as in Romans 16:25 the gospel and the preaching of Jesus Christ were in apposition to the mystery.[157] Once again, the mystery, formerly hidden, is now disclosed (I Cor. 2:7; Rom. 16:25 with the same verb). The recipients of this disclosure are the saints,[158] who are reminiscent of Paul's "mature" of I Corinthians 2:6 (also the Synoptics' "disciples"). The mystery concerns God's plan of salvation for the Gentiles as in Romans 16:25, and, indeed, is even more specifically identified with Christ. And finally, we again encounter the notion that the purpose of proclaiming the mystery is to make every man spiritually mature, the *teleios* of I Corinthians 2:6.

Among the new elements is the author's insistence on completing the message of God, on showing the *full glory* of the mysterious divine plan. The grandeur of the mystery is that Christ himself is

[156] We cannot enter the disputed question of the Pauline authorship of Colossians and Ephesians. Nevertheless, we shall point out in detail the similarities in the use of *mystērion* to that of the earlier Pauline epistles.

In both Colossians and Ephesians *oikonomia* appears in the *mystērion* passages and is always hard to translate. Prümm, "Mystères," (cited above, n. 45), cols. 208-09: "The meaning of the word oscillates between assignment, prearranged plan, and the execution of a prearranged plan." Reumann, "*Oikonomia*-terms" (cited above, n. 136), pp. 162-63, points out that in the present passage *oikonomia* is followed significantly by *tou Theou*, so that it is not simply a task assigned by God to Paul but a role in God's revealed plan.

[157] Cf. also I Cor. 2:1 compared with 1:24 (p. 49 above). For another example of the apposition between *mystērion* and *logos*, compare the mystery passage I Cor. 15:51 with I Thess. 4:15, "For we say this to you in a message (*logos*) from the Lord, that we who are still left alive at the coming of Christ will by no means come before those who have died."

[158] L. Cerfaux, *The Church in the Theology of St. Paul* (New York: Herder, 1959), pp. 130-40, concludes that the "saints" refer to a particular group: the Pentecostal community of Jerusalem. C. Masson, *Ephésiens* ("Commentaire du NT," 9; Neuchâtel and Paris, 1953), p. 173, n. 5, holds that the "saints" of Colossians are the same as the apostles and prophets of Eph. 3:5.

among the Colossians.[159] Since this Christ who dwells among them is the Christ who is supreme over all things (1:15-18) and in whom the fullness of God is present (1:19), the presence of Christ gives the Colossians their hope of glory.[160] The stress on the greatness of the divine salvific plan and on Christ's role in it must be understood in the light of the difficulty besetting the Colossians who gave undue importance to the role of the angels.[161] The author wants them to realize that in the divine mystery Christ alone suffices to give them the hope of glory.

This is even clearer in the next mystery passage (2:2) where the author says he is striving for all Christians:[162]

(2) in order that their hearts may take courage and be knit together in love, and [that they may attain] unto all the riches of the fullness of understanding, unto the knowledge of *the mystery of God*, Christ, (3) in whom are hidden all the treasures of wisdom and knowledge.

Here the knowledge of the mystery is associated with Christian love. This agrees with earlier Pauline ideas: the Spirit of God who works in the heart to bring about an understanding of the full effects of God's salvation (I Cor. 2:7-10) is the same Spirit who joins hearts in love. As for the breathless apposition, "the mystery of God, Christ," we must realize that the author is not identifying the mystery with a static picture of Christ, but with the salvific Christ, the Redeemer of Jew and Gentile.[163] We must further ob-

---

[159] Mitton, *Ephesians* (cited above, n. 125), p. 88, insists that in this passage the emphasis on Christ and his indwelling overshadows the inclusion of the Gentiles. It is not certain, however, whether the "Christ, *en hymin*" is to be taken as "among you" or "in you" in a mystical sense.

[160] The element of ultimate glory again connects the grasp of the mystery with spiritual growth; it is a question of the *approfondissement* (deepening) of the divine plan through the Spirit, and this leads towards glory (Schneider [cited above, n. 27], p. 270). On *doxa,* cf. C. F. D. Moule, *Epistles to Colossians and Philemon* ("Cambridge Greek Testament," 1957), pp. 83-4.

[161] In Col. 2:8 Paul warns them not to go astray in reference to "the elemental spirits of the universe." In 2:18 Paul attacks the worship of the angels.

[162] For the phrase in v. 2, "the mystery of God, Christ," there are many variants, none of which materially affects Paul's meaning. Our rendering does not seem so curt if we remember that it presupposes the details in the previous chapter of the epistle about the mystery of the indwelling of Christ among the Gentiles (cf. C. Masson, *Colossiens* ["Commentaire du NT," 10; Neuchâtel and Paris, 1950], p. 118).

[163] Schneider (cited above, n. 27), p. 269; Deden (cited above, n. 1), p. 408. Werner Bieder, "Das Geheimnis des Christus nach dem Epheserbrief," *Theologische Zeitschrift*, 11 (1955), pp. 335-36: "One cannot think of this Christ without his body, which encloses in itself Jew and Gentile."

serve the totality emphasized in this passage: the mystery of Christ is "the riches of the fullness of understanding"; it contains all the hidden treasures of wisdom and knowledge. In other words, the Colossians need not seek beyond Christ.[164] And once again wisdom is connected with the mystery. In I Corinthians 2:7 the hidden (*apokekrymmenē*) wisdom of God was *en mystēriō*; in Colossians 1:28 the role is reversed, for Paul proclaims the hidden (*apokekrymmenon*) mystery of Christ *en pasē sophia*. And in Colossians 2:3 the mystery of Christ contains wisdom.

The final occurrence of *mystērion* is Colossians 4:3, where the author exhorts the people to pray for him:

(3) . . . that God may open a door to us for [preaching] the message (*logos*), for declaring the *mystery* of Christ because of which I am imprisoned.

Once again we find *logos* and *mystērion* in apposition. And, indeed, this text brings out the intimate connection between God's plan of salvation and apostolic evangelizing: the former is the object of the latter; the latter puts the former into effect.

We may now treat together the Jewish parallels to the new aspects of the mystery brought forth in all three passages of Colossians. The chief feature to be considered here is the application of "mystery" to the person of Christ (albeit in a somewhat extended manner which includes the actions of his life). Naturally, granted the uniqueness of Christ's role in the Christian theology of salvation, we cannot expect an exact parallel in Jewish writings. But we have something similar in Enoch 48:6; 51:3; and 62:7, where the Elect One, the Son of Man, the light of the nations (notice that the Gentiles are involved, as in Colossians), was chosen and hidden in God's presence before creation (the mystery of Christ was hidden from ages past). But in the day of the judgment, God shall reveal

164 Although what is said about the mystery of Christ to the Colossians is explicable against the background of the Semitic concept of mystery and has parallels in previous Pauline passages, it is not impossible that the mystery terminology of this letter is meant to counter the Colossian heretics who had reshaped Christianity in the image of a mystery cult (cf. 2:23, and G. Bornkamm, "Die Häresie des Kolosserbriefes," *Theologische Literaturzeitung*, 73 [1948], cols. 11-20, reprinted in *Das Ende des Gesetzes: Paulusstudien* ["Beiträge zur evangelischen Theologie," 16; Munich: Kaiser, 4th ed., 1963], pp. 139-56).

him to the elect (Colossians: "to the saints"), and his mouth shall pour forth all the secrets of wisdom and counsel (the mystery of Christ contains all the treasures of wisdom and knowledge).[165] As a result there ensues the blessedness of the just (Colossians: the hope of glory). Of course, there is no suggestion that Enoch's Elect One, often considered a messianic figure, saves men through personal salvific activity, but the similarity of vocabulary and concept is still interesting.[166]

Other features of the *mystērion* in Colossians will be treated in considering Ephesians, but we might note a few parallels in vocabulary between Qumran and Colossians. In 2:2 the author speaks of knowledge (*epignōsis*) of the mystery of God. A favorite Qumran expression is "to give knowledge in the marvelous mysteries of God" —*hwdy' bswd* or *brzy pl'*.[167] Again in 2:3 the mystery of Christ contains wisdom and knowledge; Qumran speaks of the "mysteries of divine wisdom or insight"—*rzy śkl* (1QH 12:13; 13:13-14), and the "mysteries of knowledge"—*rzy d't* (1QS 4:6). And we may recall 1QH 2:9-10: "You have set me up as . . . a *swd* of truth and understanding to those whose path is righteous." Finally, while for Colossians the mystery of Christ is the hope of glory, in 1QS 11:5-8 the marvelous mysteries of God are "a fountain of glory."

7. THE EPISTLE TO THE EPHESIANS

Even those who deny its Pauline authorship admit the importance of this epistle for NT theology and the development of the thought of the Pauline school. This is particularly true for the study of the *mystērion*, which occurs six times. The first passage is Eph. 1:9. Praising God because in Jesus he has blessed the world and redeemed man, the writer says:

(7) . . . according to the richness of his grace, (8) which he has caused to abound in us in all wisdom and prudence, (9) having made known to us *the mystery of his will*, according to his good pleasure

[165] The Ethiopic words in Enoch 51:3 are *ṭebab* and *ḥelīnā*. The Ethiopic NT translates the *sophia* and *gnōsis* of Col. 2:3 by *ṭebab* and *meker*.

[166] See also 1QH 5:11: "You, O my God, have hidden me from the sons of men . . . until the time of the revelation of your salvation to me." In the obscure Qumran parable in 1QH 8, a person who plays a special role in God's plan for the community seems to be spoken of in terms of "hidden" and "mystery"—see above, pp. 26–27.

[167] 1QH 4:27-28; 7:27; 11:9. In 1QH 2:13; 12:13 we have the noun *d't* (*brzy pl'*).

which he has set forth in him [Christ] (10) for carrying out in the fullness of time—to gather together all things in Christ, both heavenly and earthly in him.

We encounter here some familiar notions. Once again wisdom is connected with the revelation of the mystery.[168] The wisdom and prudence which accompany God's kindness in making known the mystery in Eph. 1:8 resemble the wisdom and knowledge hidden in the mystery in Col. 2:3. In Eph. 1:10 *oikonomia* ("carrying out") again enters the sphere of the mystery as in Col. 1:25. In Col. 1:27 the indwelling of Christ among the Gentiles manifested the richness of glory (*to ploutos tēs doxēs*) of the mystery, and supplied the hope of glory. In Eph. 1:7 the revelation of the mystery is a manifestation of the richness of divine grace (*to ploutos tēs charitos*), and in v. 14 we hear that the whole purpose of the calling of the Gentiles is for the praise of divine glory.

Before we comment in detail on Ephesians 1, we wish to present the three references to *mystērion* in Ephesians 3—the most complete treatment of the mystery in the Pauline epistles. The author speaks to the Gentiles:

(2) If indeed you have even heard of the administration (*oikonomia*) of the grace of God which was given me for you: (3) how he made known to me by revelation *the mystery* (see my brief observations above—(4) from them you can see what insight I have in *the mystery of Christ*) (5) which in previous generations was not made known to men, as it has now been revealed to his holy apostles and prophets in Spirit: (6) the Gentiles are admitted to the same heritage and to the same body, and are beneficiaries of the same promise in Jesus Christ by means of the gospel (7) of which I became a servant. . . . (8) To me, the most insignificant of all the saints, was given the grace to announce to the Gentiles the unsearchable riches of Jesus Christ, (9) and to show clearly to all the working out (*oikonomia*) of *the mystery* which has been hidden from ages in the God who created all things, (10) so that the many-faceted wisdom of God now has been

---

[168] The phrase "in all wisdom and prudence" could even be translated with the "having made known" of v. 9; but on the basis of the parallel in Col. 1:9 we agree with Masson, *Ephésiens* (cited above, n. 158), p. 144, that the phrase is better situated in v. 8. We might note with J. T. Trinidad, "The Mystery Hidden in God," *Biblica*, 31 (1950), p. 17, that the relation of wisdom to mystery is not always the same in Paul: sometimes wisdom is the mystery itself; sometimes it is an attribute produced in Christians by participation in the mystery.

made known to the principalities and the powers in the heavenly places through the church, (11) according to the eternal design which he has realized in Jesus Christ, our Lord.

There are many familiar expressions here. *Oikonomia* occurs twice,[169] once governing *mystērion* as *oikonomos* did in I Cor. 4:1. We hear again that the mystery is *apokekrymmenon* (v. 9) as in I Cor. 2:7 and Col. 1:26. Once more there is a selectivity of the group to whom the mystery was first revealed (see I Cor. 2:6; Col. 1:26): the apostles and prophets.[170] In v. 5 the role of the Spirit is mentioned as it was in I Cor. 2:10; 14:2; and Eph. 1:13.

Now we turn to the very difficult question of the real content of the mystery in these two passages from Ephesians. The second passage is the easier, for 3:6 gives the definition of the mystery mentioned in 3:3: it is the inclusion of the Gentiles in God's salvific plan, i.e., the same idea we found in Rom. 16:26 and Col. 1:25-27. The gospel is mentioned in 3:6 as instrumental in bringing about the participation of the Gentiles, also a facet encountered before. As for the phrase, "the mystery of Christ," mentioned in the parenthesis of 3:4,[171] we have seen the same expression in Col. 4:3. Thus

---

169 Reumann, *"Oikonomia*-terms" (cited above, n. 136), p. 164, shows that in both instances the term covers not only God's plan but also God's administering activity in carrying out that plan. J. T. Sanders, "Hymnic Elements in Ephesians 1-3," *ZNW*, 56 (1965), pp. 214-32, thinks that in Ephesians 3 the concept of *oikonomia* from Colossians has been redefined in terms of the rule that the Gentiles also belong to the church. Reumann, p. 165, n. 4, does not share this view.

170 It is generally understood that the prophets here are figures of NT times endowed with charismatic gifts. We wonder, however, if OT prophets could not be meant: the "now" could govern the apostles, and the *en pneumati* could refer to the manner of revelation to the OT prophets (see Robinson, *Ephesians* [cited above, n. 27], p. 78 for *en pneumati* as a spiritual process). This would then be the same idea as Rom. 16:26. We call attention to the already cited Sirach 48:24-25, where the prophet Isaiah foresaw mysteries "through a great spirit."

171 Mitton, *Ephesians* (cited above, n. 125), p. 89, argues that while in Colossians the mystery is identified with Christ, this is not true of Ephesians. Yet when this same phrase, "the mystery of Christ," occurs in Col. 4:3, Mitton understands it to mean "the mystery consisting in Christ." Why should it not mean the same in Ephesians? Again Mitton claims that while Colossians associates the mystery with *logos* or the message of God (1:25; 4:3), Ephesians does not. However, the *"logos"* of truth, the gospel of salvation" of Eph. 1:13, in its context, refers back to the mystery of Eph. 1:9. Any attempt to prove from a difference in ideas on *mystērion* that the same author did not write Colossians and Ephesians is, in our opinion, precarious.

the *mystērion* presented in Eph. 3 contains many of the same aspects seen in Romans and Colossians.[172]

The mystery passage of Eph. 1, however, does seem to add a new ,element to the Pauline *mystērion*. Here the mysterious plan is to gather together[173] all things on heaven and earth in Christ. Naturally this attempt to express the totality of the mystery must be interpreted in the light of the context of the epistle. The simple explanation that it means that all men are to be affected by the salvation of Christ[174] does not seem adequate: it does not explain why all things both *in heaven* and on earth are included. The rest of this first chapter[175] gives us a better suggestion for the "heavenly things" which are subject to Christ. Here it is emphasized that Christ is in heaven above all principalities, powers, and dominions (which are themselves in heavenly places—6:12), so that all things are at his feet. We are back to the same argument that we met in Colossians: the argument that Christ is superior to the angels. The author seems to have in mind the view that before the coming of Christ, men were subject to the angels, good and bad. But now all things are subject to Christ, even the angels. Some of these angelic powers still strive for domination, and struggle against the church (Eph. 6:12) ; but the fact that Christ has been made head over them for the church (1:22) guarantees the church's victory. In this interpretation, the mystery of the divine will in Eph. 1:9-10 is a picture of the final stage of the divine *oikonomia*: the fullness of time

[172] Masson, no upholder of Pauline authorship, says (*Ephésiens* [cited above, n. 158], pp. 177-78) that the mystery is the same in Ephesians and Colossians, except that Ephesians is more complete. So also Schneider (cited above, n. 27), p. 272, n. 3. J. T. Sanders (cited above, n. 169), once more sees Eph. 3 as redefining the terminology of Colossians: now *mystērion* has become a principle of church order revealed only to the Jewish Christian Church leaders, so that this hierarchy becomes the gracious dispenser to the Gentiles of the right of membership in the body of Christ. Obviously this differs from our interpretation of the *mystērion* in Ephesians.

[173] The verb is *anakephalaiōsasthai*; the translation "to bring under one head" is satisfactory, provided it is noted that the verb is a denominative from *kephalaion*, "main point, synopsis," and not from *kephalē*, "head." Of course, the writer himself may have connected it with *kephalē*, which is a word prominent in Pauline thought (Dupont, *Gnosis* [cited above, n. 124], p. 425.

[174] This is close to the opinion of Trinidad (cited above, n. 168), pp. 19-20. For a critique which affects Trinidad's whole interpretation of this chapter, especially vv. 12-13, see Masson, *Ephésiens* (cited above, n. 158), p. 146, and Bieder (cited above, n. 163), pp. 333-34.

[175] Prümm, "Mystères" (cited above, n. 45), col. 206, shows that 1:15-23, although it does not use the word *mystērion*, is a development of the mystery idea of 1:9. In these lines there are similarities of vocabulary to the mystery passages of I Corinthians.

wherein men on earth and the angels are all subject to Christ. From the eternal point of view, this mystery of complete subjection to Christ exists already, for Christ has come and evil is vanquished; from the temporal view, the Christians are locked in struggle with the forces of evil to bring about the perfect headship of Christ.

This interpretation of the mystery in Eph. 1 greatly clarifies 3:10, where it is stated that the mystery "has now been made known to, the principalities and the powers through the church." The angelic powers see now that their authority is ended and that, according to God's plan, all things are subject to Christ. The establishment of the church, which is the working out of the divine mystery, is the tangible evidence of this.[176]

Now how does this cosmic and eschatological interpretation of the mystery in Eph. 1[177] fit in with the concept of mystery in the other Pauline epistles? The ideas are in harmony with those of Colossians, although the connection between Christ's supremacy over the heavenly powers and the mystery of salvation is more explicit in Ephesians. Yet, even in Colossians, the Christ who is the mystery (1:27) is described thus (1:16): "In him was created everything *which is in heaven and on earth*, visible and invisible, whether thrones or dominions or principalities or powers—all things were created through him and *for him*. He is above all things, and all

---

[176] Prümm, "Mystères" (cited above, n. 45), col. 209: "In the eyes of men the church concretizes the mystery." This interpretation of "through the church" seems more probable than that of Schneider (cited above, n. 27), pp. 271-72, who maintains that because the church, the body of Christ, is in heaven above the angelic powers, the mystery is first revealed to the church, and then through the church to the powers who are not members of Christ.

[177] We would call attention to Werner Bieder's explanation (cited above, n. 163) of the Ephesian mystery which resembles ours in many details, but brings in some notions for which we find little support. For instance, he gives *ta panta* in 1:10, which we interpret in the general sense of the whole of creation (so also Masson, *Colossiens* [cited above, n. 162], p. 99, n. 4), a much more precise meaning. The "All" is the confused and leaderless division, in strife with God and one another, under the domination of the powers and dominions (p. 343, notes 47-8) which in Ephesians is dualistically opposed to the church. The *mystērion* signifies the divine will which is made public in the dominion of Jesus Christ over the All, and which calls the Church composed of Jews and Gentiles to share in this dominion. But is there sufficient evidence for such a concept of *ta panta* as a separate class? It demands less of the imagination to see the "All" as the totality of creation, including the angelic powers both good and bad. Of course, to some extent, one's interpretation of *ta panta* depends on whether or not one posits gnostic influence on the thought of those to whom the epistle is directed.

things are brought together in him." Ephesians 1:10 brings these two verses from Col. 1 together.

When we go beyond Colossians, however, we must admit that the concept of mystery is more developed in the Captivity Epistles than it is in II Thessalonians, I Corinthians, or Romans. Nevertheless, we would be slow to assume that this development is not Paul's, since it is certainly not out of harmony with the use of *mystērion* in the earlier epistles.[178] II Thessalonians and I Cor. 15:51 show a strong eschatological element in the mystery; I Cor. 2:8 mentions that the mystery was hidden from the rulers of this world, now doomed; totality is a key note in many of the earlier mystery passages.[179] These traces of the ideas found in Colossians and Ephesians, plus the many vocabulary similarities already pointed out, make conclusions about difference of authorship most hazardous.

After this long but necessary discussion, we turn at last to the Semitic parallels for Eph. 1 and 3. Beginning with vocabulary, we see that in 3:4 Paul speaks of his "insight" (*synesis*) in the mystery. At Qumran, we find the expression "to give insight into the mysteries"—*hśkyl brzm*.[180] It is interesting that Colossians speaks of *epignōsis* while Ephesians speaks of *synesis*. Qumran has parallels for both in *hwdy'* and *hśkyl*, used with "mysteries"; and in 1QH 11:9-10 we find *hwdy' bswd* and *hśkyl brzm* used in parallelism—the Hebrew equivalents of the two different words used in Colossians and Ephesians! Another point is that in the definition of mystery in Eph. 3:6 Paul for the first time mentions the admission of the Gentiles to the same heritage (*synklēronoma*). In treating I Cor. 2:7 (see p. 43 above) we called attention to the remarkable Qumran passage 1QS 11:5-8 and its affinities with the Pauline concept of mystery. We note here that its last line sums up what has been said of the mysteries and of the wisdom and glory which God entrusted to Qumran: "God has granted these to those whom he elected as an eternal possession, and has constituted them an *inheritance* in the lot of the saints." Again Eph. 1:9 speaks of "the mystery of God's will"; we might compare this to Qumran's *rzy ḥpṣ* (1QH Frag. 3:7)—"the mysteries of God's good pleasure."

[178] Robinson, *Ephesians* (cited above, n. 27), p. 238: "The use of the word which we find in the Epistles to the Colossians and the Ephesians is no new one."

[179] E.g., I Cor. 15:51, we shall *all* be transformed; Rom. 11:26, *all* Israel shall be saved; Rom. 16:26, *all* the Gentiles shall be led to the obedience of faith.

[180] 1QH 12:20; 1QS 9:18. In the LXX *synesis* with some form of *didōmi* often renders *hśkyl*, e.g., Dan. 1:17.

The purpose of the revelation of the mystery in Eph. 1:12, 14 is ultimately "for the praise of his glory"; in 1QH 13:13-14 we hear: "And in the mysteries of your wisdom you have divi[ded?] all these things to make your glory known."

The hidden nature of the mystery has some interesting features in Eph. 3:9. It is said to be hidden "from the ages in the God who created all things." As Masson points out,[181] this is a typical idea in Jewish apocalyptic: the eschatological mysteries already exist in heaven, and have only to be unveiled. In Enoch 103:2 we have the mysteries on heavenly tablets; and the Son of Man in Enoch 48:6 and 62:7 was hidden *in the presence of God* before creation. Eph. 3:10 states that the mysterious plan of God was hitherto unknown to angelic powers. This is not strange to the Jewish concept of divine mysteries. Enoch 16:3 (following the Greek) says of the evil angels that, before they lost heaven, not all the mysteries had been revealed to them. And even the good angels do not know the "secret name" of Enoch 69:14. And several times we have heard that God alone knows all the mysteries (II Baruch 48:2-3; 54:1).

So much for the minor points. We may now turn to the question of a Semitic background for the *haut motif* of the Ephesian mystery: that in Christ all things in heaven and on earth are summed up. We shall do this from the viewpoint of the object of the author's attack: the theory of the angelic domination of man.[182] It is clear that Col. 2:8-19 places this heresy among a bevy of Judaizing errors, that the titles of these angelic forces, such as "ruler," "principality,"

---

181 *Éphésiens* (cited above, n. 158), p. 177. Bornkamm, *TDNT, "mystērion"* (article cited above, n. 1), p. 816, gives this description of the mysteries found in apocalyptic works: "The mysteries are God's counsels destined finally to be disclosed. They are the final events and states which are already truly existent in heaven and may be seen there, and which will in the last days emerge from their concealment and become manifest events." On the pattern which runs through many of the Pauline *mystērion*-passages, "once hidden/now revealed," a pattern found at Eph. 3:5, 9-10; Col. 1:26; Rom. 16:25-26; cf. Eph. 1:9-10; I Cor. 2:7 ff., see Hans Conzelmann's commentary on Ephesians in *Die kleineren Briefe des Apostels Paulus* ("Das NT Deutsch," 8; Göttingen: Vandenhoeck & Ruprecht, 10th ed., 1965), pp. 71-72.

182 Previous attempts to identify this heresy have not been too successful. E. Percy, *Die Probleme der Kolosser- und Epheserbriefe* (Lund, 1946), made a minute study (pre-Qumran) of all Jewish, Greek, and Christian texts on the subject; his conclusion was that they are either inapplicable or not convincing. Of course, only if Ephesians was written at the same time as Colossians, may one draw upon Bornkamm's careful analysis of the Colossian heresy (see n. 164 above).

and "power," are derived from Jewish angelology.[183] After the Qumran discoveries, we are in a position to state that a theory of angelic domination was definitely in vogue in Jewish circles at the time of Jesus and of Paul. In 1QS 3:17 ff. it is stated that all men are under two spirits or angels (of light and darkness). Throughout the Qumran literature we see the dominion of the respective angels being exercised for or against the community, and we understand from 3:23 that this conflict of dominion is "according to the mysteries of God until the final period" (cf. Eph. 1:9—the mystery of his will carried out in the fullness of time). The final period comes in 1QM where Belial and his subsidiary angels, directing the sons of darkness and perversion (compare to Eph. 2:2, "the ruler of the power of the air, the spirit now at work in the sons of disobedience"), are defeated by the sons of light and the angels whom God sends to aid them.

While such a concept of angelic domination corresponds well to the heresy which Ephesians is opposing, we have no way of knowing whether the two are the same. But we may say that whatever the exact nature of the error attacked by Colossians and Ephesians, its features are certainly not strange to the Jewish world, as exemplified by Qumran.[184] And if for Ephesians the mystery is to subject all things in heaven and on earth to Christ, for Qumran God's mysterious plan includes control over heaven and earth. In 1QM 14:14 we hear: ". . . great is your majestic plan and your marvelous mysteries on high with you for raising up to you from the dust, and casting down from the angels."[185]

One final point should be noticed. We mentioned a certain bifurcation in the Pauline outlook on the mystery: the eternal point of

[183] See the articles on *"archē, archōn"* and on *"exousia"* respectively by G. Delling and W. Foerster in *TDNT*, 1, pp. 482-84, 488-89; 2, pp. 571-73, and the numerous references given there. Foerster, p. 571, says of these terms in their meaning of supernatural powers: "The expressions *archai* and *exousiai* are not found in Hellenism or pagan Gnosticism in this sense."

[184] Close parallels between the language and thought of Qumran and that of Colossians and Ephesians have been pointed out by many authors, especially W. D. Davies and K. G. Kuhn. For details see H. Braun, *Theologische Rundschau*, 29 (1963-64), pp. 235-53; expanded in *Qumran und das Neue Testament* (Tübingen: J. C. B. Mohr [Paul Siebeck], 1966), 1, pp. 215-33.

[185] Cf. n. 76 above. A noun from *ḥšb,* meaning "plan," is parallel to *rāz,* "mystery," here, and in 1QH 1:29-30. In 1QH Frag. 17:3 we have *rzy mḥšbt.* This matches the Pauline idea that the divine mystery is a secret plan.

view where all things are summed up in Christ, and the temporal view where a struggle is still in progress. This twofold outlook is typical of Jewish apocalyptic. While a work such as Enoch shows perfect awareness that there are struggles at hand yet to be fought, it can (61:8-10) state that the Elect One is superior to the angelic hosts of heaven and will judge them.

Having studied the two main mystery passages in Ephesians (chapters 1 and 3), we now turn to a less important usage of *mystērion* in the conclusion to the epistle, 6:19. Paul asks the prayers of the people:

(19) . . . that speech (*logos*) may be given to me when I open my mouth, boldly to make known *the mystery of the gospel*, (20) on account of which I am an ambassador in chains.

The passage closely resembles Colossians 4:3, where God is asked to give Paul an opportunity to declare freely "the mystery of Christ." To be noted is the phrase of Ephesians, "the mystery of the gospel," which occurs only here.[186] The two phrases "of Christ" and "of the gospel" are only different aspects of the same basic reality, because the gospel announces the mystery, which is salvation for all in Christ.[187] Very cleverly Werner Bieder has compared the three genitives found with *mystērion* in Ephesians: the mystery of the will of God (1:9), of Christ (3:4), and of the gospel (6:19). All three form a whole: "The mystery concerning the *divine will* which is put into effect in *Christ* and preached in the *gospel*."[188]

We have left to the end the peculiar use of *mystērion* in Ephesians 5:32. Speaking of marriage, the passage says that a man should love his wife as he does his own flesh, or indeed as Christ loves the church (for the members of the church are the members of his body). Then Genesis 2:24 is cited:

(31) "For this reason shall a man leave his father and mother and be united to his wife; and the two shall be one flesh." (32) This is a

---

186 Yet in I Cor. 2:1 we may have a close parallel (see p. 48-49 above), *katangellein to mystērion* (?). Also to be considered is Rom. 16:25, where *kata to euangelion* is parallel to *kata apokalypsin mystēriou*. The genitive "of the gospel" in our present passage is probably subjective, i.e., the gospel announcing the mystery.

187 Deden (cited above, n. 1), p. 409, points out that in a way the gospel is interchangeable with the mystery; e.g., Gal. 1:11-16 describes the gospel in the same way we have seen Ephesians describing the mystery. The mystery in itself signifies the hidden nature of the divine plan; the gospel is the external manifestation of that plan to the people affected by it.

188 Bieder (cited above, n. 163), p. 330.

profound *mystērion*, and I interpret it as referring to Christ and his Church. (33) But anyway, as far as you are concerned, let every single one of you love his wife as himself; and let the wife respect the husband.

In our interpretation, the function of the sentence containing the word *mystērion* is that of an aside. The text of Genesis which the author has just quoted fits the argument that he is presenting: a man should love his wife as he loves his own flesh. Why? Because the two are one flesh according to the Scriptures. Now the author had already introduced a second simile into his argument: a man should love his wife as Christ loves the church. Why? Because the church is Christ's body just as a man's wife is his flesh. Keeping this second simile in mind as he quotes Genesis, the author sees in the Genesis passage, in addition to the obvious meaning, a deeper, hidden meaning that refers to the relation between Christ and the church. But since he does not wish to dwell on this second simile,[189] he closes his aside and gets back to the main point.

Therefore *mystērion*, as employed in Ephesians 5:32, refers to a Scripture passage which contains a deeper meaning than that which appears at first sight.[190] We do not believe that there is any exact parallel for this use of the term in the NT.[191] (However, in the Christian writers of the second century, especially Justin, a deeper

[189] As the word *plēn* clearly indicates (see Blass-Debrunner-Funk, *A Greek Grammar of the NT* [Chicago, 1961], § 449, n. 2). Prümm, "Mystères" (cited above, n. 45), cols. 223-24, suggests that Paul had already talked enough about the mystery of Christ and the church, so that further detail would be superfluous.

[190] Bornkamm, *TDNT*, "*mystērion*" (article cited above, n. 1), p. 823: "The *mystērion* is thus the allegorical meaning of the OT saying, its mysteriously concealed prophecy of the relation of Christ to the *ekklēsia*." However, Bornkamm is on less certain ground when he says that Paul's interpretation of Genesis is opposed to some other allegorical interpretations made by representatives of a gnostic group at Ephesus. When Paul says *egō de legō*, he need not be opposing some other interpretation; he may simply mean that he himself is going beyond the obvious meaning of the passage.

[191] Hatch, *Essays* (cited above, n. 136), p. 61, and Bouyer (cited above, n. 107), p. 22, see a parallel in the Apocalypse where *mystērion* is a symbol with a hidden meaning. However, there is certainly a difference between the strange symbolic visions of the Apocalypse which have no meaning beyond what they symbolize and the relatively clear Scripture passage cited in Eph. 5:32 in which the writer sees an additional meaning. We might mention that Masson, *Ephésiens* (cited above, n. 158), p. 215, denies that Paul is citing the OT here on the grounds that there is no formula of quotation. But if we compare Ephesians with the LXX of Gen. 2:24, the Greek is word by word the same. Masson claims that copyists have conformed the two texts, but offers no proof.

sense of an OT passage, seen now to refer to Christ, is often called a *mystērion*.) There is a problem in our understanding of the *mystērion* in 5:32. Can "mystery" then be used of any such deeper meaning of an OT passage, or is it used here precisely because Christ and his church are involved? Throughout this epistle *mystērion* has concerned Christ's gathering all men to himself in the church. Is it with this in mind that the author calls the hidden reference to Christ and the church in the Genesis passage a *mystērion*?[192] We feel that the lack of evidence renders an answer impossible. We have seen too much variation of meaning in the history of the word "mystery" to argue that one writer cannot use the word with two different shades of meaning. And certainly in the Church Fathers *mystērion* is used for many different types of deeper meanings seen in the OT.[193]

When we turn to the Jewish background, we are certainly aware that the Jews themselves saw the possibility of drawing deep and hidden meaning from OT passages. The question is: did they use the term "mystery" to refer to such meanings? Sirach 39:2-7 teaches that the hidden things (*apokrypha*) of God can be found in the parables of ancient lore; but this is not a good parallel for Ephesians, since one expects parables to be enigmatic and to have hidden meaning. A better example is Qumran's idea (1QpHab. 7:1-5) that beneath the words of ancient prophecies lie mysteries (*rzm*), the meaning of which God reveals to the Teacher whom he has raised up. This is closer to the idea in Ephesians; but the Qumran search for such mysteries in a line-by-line *pešer* of the prophets, adapting every line to its own situation, is not at all the same as the Ephesian exegesis. Again for Philo, "allegorizing" was a means of obtaining the mysteries hidden in the Scriptures; but there is no close parallel between Philo's philosophical accommodations and this instance of Pauline exegesis. Thus, while what we know of the Semitic background would certainly allow a use of "mystery" such as we have seen in Ephesians 5:32, we can adduce no perfect parallel.

192 Many authors think so: Schneider (cited above, n. 27), p. 272; Bieder (cited above, n. 163), p. 336; Masson, *Ephésiens* (cited above, n. 158), p. 215.
193 For the use of *mystērion* after the NT period, see von Soden (cited above, n. 107); K. Prümm, *"Mystērion* von Paulus bis Origenes," *Zeitschrift für Katholische Theologie,* 61 (1937), pp. 391-425; Hatch, *Essays* (cited above, n. 136), pp. 60-1; Christine Mohrmann, "Sacramentum dans les plus anciens textes chrétiens," *Harvard Theological Review,* 47 (1954), pp. 141-52; and V. Loi, "Il termine 'mysterium' nella letteratura latina christiana prenicena," *Vigiliae Christianae,* 19 (1965), pp. 210-32; 20 (1966), pp. 25-44.

8. The First Epistle to Timothy

The two passages, 3:9 and 3:16, are the last examples of *mystērion* in the Pauline writings. In 3:9, after giving the qualifications of the bishop, the author[194] turns to those of the deacons who must be serious, sober, unselfish.

(9) preserving *the mystery of faith* in pure conscience.

Having finished listing the qualifications, he adds a personal note to Timothy. He says that he is writing these instructions so that, if he is delayed in coming, Timothy will know how to act fittingly in the church of God, the pillar and bulwark of truth:

(16) For assuredly, great is *the mystery of religion*:
The one who was manifested in flesh, was justified in spirit,
was seen by the angels, was preached among the Gentiles,
was believed in the world, was taken up in glory.

The meaning of the mystery of faith and of religion can be clearly seen from the context. One of the chief dangers to Timothy is from those who are teaching new doctrines and swerving from the old (1:3-7). Therefore, all the officers of the church must be drawn from those who carefully preserve the true doctrine. By "the mystery of faith," then, the author seems to mean the doctrinal content of faith. We may say that the mystery of faith is what is believed, as the mystery of the gospel is what is preached.[195] In like manner "the mystery of religion" means the object of religious adherence. But in 3:16 the short hymn[196] that follows clarifies the content of

---

[194] Once again we wish to avoid any discussion of whether the Pastoral Epistles are genuinely Pauline or deutero-Pauline. But we shall compare the use of *mystērion* here with that of other Pauline epistles.

[195] Spicq, *Épîtres Pastorales* (cited above, n. 129), p. 118. Robinson, *Ephesians* (cited above, n. 27), p. 239, points out that, from the context, no really secret doctrine can be meant here. The phrase "can only refer to such elementary and fundamental knowledge as any servant of the Church must necessarily have." Schneider, (cited above, n. 27), p. 275, observes that Paul says that the mystery of faith is to be preserved in *pure conscience*. The deacon must be purer than other men because a mystery is entrusted to him which unbelievers cannot understand because they are not pure. Once again there is a correlation between grasp of the mystery and spiritual life.

[196] Cf. E. Schweizer in *Current Issues in New Testament Interpretation* (O. Piper Festschrift; New York: Harper, 1962), pp. 166-77.

the mystery. The mystery to be adored is Christ, and Christ as incarnate, or putting into effect the divine plan of salvation (as in Colossians and Ephesians). This mystery of Christ, formerly hidden, has now been "seen by the angels" (as in Eph. 3:10). This mystery of Christ has been "preached among the Gentiles" (*passim* in the Pauline mystery passages). In this mystery the world has believed (Rom. 16:26: all the Gentiles brought to the obedience of faith). And the final theme is that in this mystery Christ is raised in glory (Eph. 1:10). Thus the mystery of religion, as unfolded in six parallel statements, sums up admirably all the aspects of the Pauline *mystērion* already seen in the other epistles.[197] And the very idea which brings on the exclamation of 3:16 about the greatness of the mystery is that of the church, mentioned in the preceding verse— the church which in Colossians and Ephesians is the tangible evidence of the realization of the mystery: the union of Jews and Gentiles in Christ's body.

We may turn now to Semitic parallels to the vocabulary of I Timothy 3:9 and 3:16. The exclamation of wonder at the greatness of the mystery reminds us of Qumran's constant expression, "the marvelous mysteries of God."[198] And Enoch 63:3 assures us that the mysteries of God are profound. For the two expressions, "the mystery of faith" and "the mystery of religion," we call attention to Enoch 58:5 where "the heritage of faith" is in apposition to "the secrets of righteousness (*hebū'āta ṣedeq*)." Now the NT word that we have translated as "religion" is *eusebeia*, which has the connotation of "godliness, piety." In the Ethiopic NT five occurrences of *eusebeia* in I Timothy are rendered by *ṣedeq*.[199] Thus the *hebū'āta ṣedeq* of our Enoch passage is a close Semitic parallel to *to tēs eusebeias mystērion* at I Tim. 3:16, a parallel heightened by a close connection with faith.

---

[197] Theodore of Beza (cited in Spicq [see above, n. 129], p. 111): "There is scarcely another passage in which all the mysteries of our redemption are more magnificently or clearly explained."

[198] Also see Sirach 43:32, "There are many mysteries yet *greater* than these."

[199] I Tim. 2:2; 4:7-8; 6:3; 6:11; and probably 6:5. Unfortunately the Ethiopic of 3:16 itself is not clear; it has these words *'amedā wadedā laṣedeq 'abiy* ("the great pillar and bulwark of righteousness") to cover the Greek: "the pillar and bulwark of truth; for assuredly great is the mystery of *eusebeia*." We cannot be certain that *ṣedeq* translates *eusebeia* here. For other examples of *hebu'āta ṣedeq* in Enoch, see 49:2; 71:3-4.

9. CONCLUSION

We have now finished our study of the NT *mystērion* passages against a Semitic background. In the total picture of the relation of NT theology to the Jewish and Hellenistic worlds, "mystery" is only one of the many questions that must be considered, and so we shall avoid sweeping conclusions. But, granted the limited nature of our field of inquiry, we have been able to draw from the Semitic world good parallels in thought and word for virtually every facet of the NT use of mystery—and this despite the fact that we possess only a fraction of the Jewish literature available to Paul. We believe it no exaggeration to say that, considering the variety and currency of the concept of divine mysteries in Jewish thought, Paul and the NT writers could have written everything they did about *mystērion* whether or not they ever encountered the pagan mystery religions. "Mystery" was a part of the native theological equipment of the Jews who came to Christ.

For Further Reading

ABOUT THE TERM "MYSTERY":

See the bibliography in the notes above, especially notes 1, 27, 45, 98-100, 107, 184, and 193.

Moule, C. F. D. "Mystery," *The Interpreter's Dictionary of the Bible* (New York and Nashville: Abingdon, 1962), 3, pp. 479-81.

BY RAYMOND E. BROWN:

"The History and Development of the Theory of a *Sensus Plenior*," *CBQ*, 15 (1953), pp. 141-62.

The Sensus Plenior of Sacred Scripture. Baltimore: St. Mary's University, 1955.

"The *Sensus Plenior* in the Last Ten Years," *CBQ*, 25 (1963), pp. 262-85.

New Testament Essays. "Impact Books." Milwaukee: Bruce Publishing Company, 1965. Collected essays on the Bible and ecumenism, the Fourth Gospel, and the Synoptics. Includes "Ecumenism and New Testament Research" (pp. 17-35), originally published in the *Journal of Ecumenical Studies*, 1 (1964), pp. 299-314, and "The Unity and Diversity in New Testament Ecclesiology," an address at the 1963 Faith and Order Conference, also published in *Novum Testamentum*, 6 (1963), pp. 298-308. This volume of essays has now been reprinted in the Doubleday Image series of paperbacks (D251; New York, 1968).

The Gospel According to John (i-xii): Introduction, Translation, and Notes. "The Anchor Bible," 29. Garden City, N.Y.: Doubleday, 1966.

Jesus: God and Man: Modern Biblical Reflections. "Impact Books." Milwaukee: Bruce Publishing Company, 1967. (Paperback ed. available.)

"After Bultmann, What? An Introduction to the Post-Bultmannians," *CBQ*, 26 (1964), pp. 1-30.

"Second Thoughts: X. The Dead Sea Scrolls and the New Testament," *Expository Times*, 78 (1966-67), pp. 19-23.

"We Profess One Baptism for the Forgiveness of Sins," *Worship*, 40 (1966), pp. 260-71. A paper prepared for the national Lutheran-Catholic dialogue.

Editor, with J. A. Fitzmyer and R. E. Murphy. *The Jerome Biblical Commentary.* Englewood Cliffs: Prentice Hall, 1968.

Facet Books Already Published

Biblical Series:

1. *The Significance of the Bible for the Church*
   by Anders Nygren (translated by Carl Rasmussen). 1963
2. *The Sermon on the Mount*
   by Joachim Jeremias (translated by Norman Perrin). 1963
3. *The Old Testament in the New* by C. H. Dodd. 1963
4. *The Literary Impact of the Authorized Version*
   by C. S. Lewis. 1963
5. *The Meaning of Hope* by C. F. D. Moule. 1963
6. *Biblical Problems and Biblical Preaching* by C. K. Barrett. 1964
7. *The Genesis Accounts of Creation* by Claus Westerman
   (translated by Norman E. Wagner). 1964
8. *The Lord's Prayer*
   by Joachim Jeremias (translated by John Reumann). 1964
9. *Only to the House of Israel? Jesus and the Non-Jews*
   by T. W. Manson. 1964
10. *Jesus and the Wilderness Community at Qumran*
    by Ethelbert Stauffer (translated by Hans Spalteholz). 1964
11. *Corporate Personality in Ancient Israel*
    by H. Wheeler Robinson. 1964
12. *The Sacrifice of Christ* by C. F. D. Moule. 1964
13. *The Problem of the Historical Jesus*
    by Joachim Jeremias (translated by Norman Perrin). 1964
14. *A Primer of Old Testament Text Criticism*
    by D. R. Ap-Thomas. 1966
15. *The Bible and the Role of Women*
    by Krister Stendahl (translated by Emilie T. Sander). 1966
16. *Introduction to Pharisaism* by W. D. Davies. 1967
17. *Man and Nature in the New Testament* by C. F. D. Moule. 1967
18. *The Lord's Supper According to the New Testament*
    by Eduard Schweizer (translated by James M. Davis). 1967
19. *The Psalms: A Form-Critical Introduction*
    by Herman Gunkel (translated by Thomas Horner). 1967
20. *The Spirit-Paraclete in the Fourth Gospel*
    by Hans Windisch (translated by James W. Cox). 1968
21. *The Semitic Background of the Term "Mystery" in the New Testament* by Raymond E. Brown, S.S. 1968

Social Ethics Series:

1. *Our Calling*
   by Einar Billing (translated by Conrad Bergendoff). 1965
2. *The World Situation* by Paul Tillich. 1965
3. *Politics as a Vocation* by Max Weber (translated by H. H. Gerth
   and C. Wright Mills). 1965
4. *Christianity in a Divided Europe* by Hanns Lilje. 1965
5. *The Bible and Social Ethics* by Hendrik Kraemer. 1965
6. *Christ and the New Humanity* by C. H. Dodd. 1965

71

7. *What Christians Stand For in the Secular World*
   by William Temple. 1965
8. *Legal Responsibility and Moral Responsibility*
   by Walter Moberly. 1965
9. *The Divine Command: A New Perspective on Law and Gospel*
   by Paul Althaus (translated by Franklin Sherman). 1966
10. *The Road to Peace* by John C. Bennett, Kenneth Johnstone,
    C. F. von Weizsacker, Michael Wright. 1966
11. *The Idea of a Natural Order: With an Essay on Modern
    Asceticism* by V. A. Demant. 1966
12. *Kerygma, Eschatology, and Social Ethics*
    by Amos N. Wilder. 1966
13. *Affluence and the Christian*
    by Hendrik van Oyen (translated by Frank Clarke). 1966
14. *Luther's Doctrine of the Two Kingdoms*
    by Heinrich Bornkamm (translated by Karl H. Hertz). 1966
15. *Christian Decision in the Nuclear Age* by T. R. Milford. 1967
16. *Law and Gospel*
    by Werner Elert (translated by Edward H. Schroeder). 1967
17. *On Marriage*
    by Karl Barth (translated by A. T. Mackay *et al.*). 1968

Historical Series:
1. *Were Ancient Heresies Disguised Social Movements?*
   by A. H. M. Jones. 1966
2. *Popular Christianity and the Early Theologians*
   by H. J. Carpenter. 1966
3. *Tithing in the Early Church*
   by Lukas Vischer (translated by Robert C. Schultz). 1966
4. *Jerusalem and Rome*
   by Hans von Campenhausen and Henry Chadwick. 1966
5. *The Protestant Quest for a Christian America 1830-1930*
   by Robert T. Handy. 1967
6. *The Formation of the American Catholic Minority 1820-1860*
   by Thomas T. McAvoy. 1967
7. *A Critical Period in American Religion 1875-1900*
   by Arthur M. Schlesinger, Sr. 1967
8. *Images of Religion in America* by Jerald C. Brauer. 1967
9. *The American Religious Depression 1925-1935*
   by Robert T. Handy. 1968
10. *The Origins of Fundamentalism: Toward a Historical Inter-
    pretation* by Ernest R. Sandeen. 1968